THE
NON-PROFIT
SECTOR
IN
SOUTH
AFRICA

ZANE DANGOR

AND THE

**DEVELOPMENT
RESOURCES CENTRE**

CAF
INTERNATIONAL

© 1997 Charities Aid Foundation

Published by Charities Aid Foundation
Kings Hill
West Malling
Kent ME19 4TA

Tel +44 (0)1732 520000
Fax +44 (0)1732 520001
Web address http://www.charitynet.org
E-mail cafpubs@caf.charitynet.org

Editor Caroline Hartnell
Design and production Eugenie Dodd Typographics
Printed and bound by Bell & Bain Ltd, Glasgow

A catalogue record for this book is available
from the British Library.

ISBN 1–85934–024–5

If you would like to know more about CAF's activities
in South Africa, please contact Paddy Ross at the
Charities Aid Foundation.

Contents

Foreword

Not so long ago, in 1993, when there was still a clear demarcation between those forces in South Africa that sought a total transformation of society and those that stood against it, the non-profit sector occupied an important role in society. It played a crucial part in attempting to address the apartheid state's developmental omissions and misapplication of development resources. The sector made a significant contribution to the preparations for the historic 1994 elections.

An important question that should be asked is: what is the state of the non-profit sector post elections and in the mid-1990s? At present, the sector is in a desperate state. It is finding that funds that were easily accessible in the apartheid era are now not so accessible. This is so despite reports in the media as well as by international donors that funding has increased. On the other hand, the development needs of communities have not decreased. The Transitional National Development Trust (TNDT), set up in an attempt to address the needs of non-profit organizations, has received more than 800 funding requests totalling R1.5 billion (US$330 million). The TNDT received only R135 million ($29 million) from the government and the European Union combined.

The response from government on the plight of the non-profit sector is not audible enough. The sector needs to realign itself to the realities of the day, in particular to the traumas of transition with its ever-changing nature. In short, the sector must take an honest audit of itself with regard to the real value it can add to the development of the new South Africa.

This publication is a breath of fresh air needed to elucidate the contemporary development terrain. It is an important contribution that is user-friendly and useful to donors, government departments and the non-profit sector itself.

E Molobi
Chairman, Kagiso Trust Investment Company

Preface

One of the main challenges facing South Africa today is to ensure that the socio-economic legacy of apartheid is addressed effectively. No political settlement can by itself bring lasting peace and development. All South Africans should have a right to equal opportunities. This means more than the government making a political commitment; all sectors of society need to take responsibility for achieving this. For this reason, redistribution and development should remain on top of the policy agenda in South Africa.

It has been widely accepted that the key economic issues revolve around the twin objectives of growth and redistribution. The Reconstruction and Development Programme (RDP), published in 1994, and the Growth, Employment and Redistribution Strategy (GEARS – also known as the Macro-Economic Strategy), introduced by the Government of National Unity in 1996, represent an attempt to balance the imperatives of sustainable internal growth with external constraints. These constraints are a consequence of trade liberalization as South Africa enters the world economy after decades of apartheid-imposed isolation. While the RDP rightfully emphasized the provision of basic services such as housing, health care and education and envisaged an active role for government in meeting these basic needs, this view appears to be in conflict with the imperatives of GEARS. This economic framework emphasizes economic growth guided by fiscal discipline and a commitment to reduce government's role in the economy.

The interplay between the government's policy of providing for basic needs and its overarching economic plan, which naturally militates against government intervention, will determine how the following development concerns are met:

- provision of primary health care, education and housing for all South Africans;
- land distribution and rural development;
- employment creation and the economic empowerment of the black majority;
- violence prevention and conflict resolution;
- protection of the environment;
- promotion of a human rights culture.

In all these areas, the focus must be on community empowerment and institutional transformation. The RDP emphasized that government, the private sector and the non-profit sector would all have vital contributions to make – and this has been accepted by government spokespeople subsequently.

The report starts with a brief overview of South Africa today: its people, its government and the prevailing social and economic situation. It then looks at the non-profit sector. In particular, it considers the needs of the sector and the contribution that foreign donors can make. Finally, the Gazetteer section covers 11 specific areas of non-profit sector activity.

This report can provide no more than an introduction to South Africa's non-profit sector and the role it can play in tackling the social and economic legacy of apartheid. It must be emphasized, however, that South Africa is in a state of transition – as it will be for many years. The report gives a picture of South African non-profit organizations at a particular point in time, but the changing economic and political environment inevitably means that the sector will develop and change in many ways over the years ahead.

The list of useful organizations may be helpful to readers wishing to find out more. Short case studies throughout the text include contact addresses, telephone and fax numbers, and e-mail addresses.

It is hoped that this publication will be of particular interest to foreign donors – whether foundations, companies or individuals – who are considering making a contribution to South Africa's development through supporting its non-profit sector.

Collection of the data

The Development Resources Centre conducted a survey of South African non-profit organizations (NPOs) for this report. Questionnaires were sent out to 1,000 NPOs asking, among other things, about their activities, funding sources, income, staff and volunteers. Only 108 organizations responded, and some of the survey findings conflict with those of an earlier survey carried out by the DRC in 1993. These discrepancies underline the fact that the non-profit sector as a whole is not reliably documented; a body of information is being built up gradually.

Definition of the non-profit sector

Mary Honey and David Bonbright, in a 1993 paper on *The Definition and Typology of NGOs*, defined non-profit organizations (NPOs) as 'private, self-governing, voluntary, non-profit-distributing organizations operating not for commercial purposes but in the public interest, for the promotion of social welfare and development, religion, charity, education and research'.

Private NPOs are neither part of the government nor governed by boards controlled or appointed by government officials. This does not mean that they may not receive significant government support or that government officials cannot sit on their boards.

Self-governing NPOs control their own activities. They have their own internal procedures for governance and are not controlled by outside entities.

Voluntary This implies some meaningful degree of voluntary participation, either in the actual conduct of the NPO's activities or in the management of its affairs. This does not mean that all or most of its income must come from voluntary contributions, or that most of its staff must be voluntary. The presence of some voluntary input, for example a voluntary board of directors, is sufficient. In practice, the financial and human resources of the organization often derive mainly from voluntary contributions.

Non-profit-distributing This means not returning profits to the members of the organization – a key distinction from private businesses. An NPO may accumulate profits in a given year, but the profits must be ploughed back into furthering its objectives.

In the public interest The NPO must operate in the public interest. This definition could be expanded upon to specify that action to benefit certain classes, such as the poor and disadvantaged, is in the public interest. Organizations that claim to operate in the public interest are accountable to that public.

Organization This means an established or permanent institution. This is demonstrated by some degree of organizational permanence, like regular meetings, officers or rules of procedure. It does not require legal incorporation or registration.

About the authors

This report was prepared and written by members of the Participatory Advocacy Department of the Development Resources Centre (DRC).

Zane Dangor is manager of the Participatory Advocacy Department. Over the last three years he has been involved in initiatives to reform the laws and policies affecting the non-profit sector in order to make them more enabling. He also helped organize and launch the South African National NGO Coalition, which is set to become one of the foremost advocates on social development issues in South Africa. Zane previously worked for the National Union of Mineworkers (NUM), where he was part of a unit that assisted former mineworkers and their families to set up cooperatives and other income-generating projects.

He is currently completing his masters degree in Public and Development Management through the Faculty of Management at the University of The Witwatersrand in Johannesburg.

Owen Stuurman is the senior advocacy officer at the DRC. Prior to taking up this position, he was the coordinator of the Ubuntu Social Development Institute; he has earned respect throughout South Africa as a trainer and facilitator of learning events. As a specialist in community-level organization, he brings to the DRC team a particular focus on advocacy training, which strengthens the organization's initiatives towards creating a more enabling environment for the non-profit sector.

Tlalane Lesoetsa is a senior researcher at the DRC. She holds an honours degree in Psychology and a diploma as a Human Sciences Researcher; she has completed the coursework component of her masters degree in Development Studies. In 1994 Tlalane worked as an intern at the Agriculture and Rural Development Research Institute (ARDRI); in 1995 she was a researcher for the Human Sciences Research Council (HSRC).

Acknowledgements

The authors wish to thank Gavin Andersson, the Executive Director of the DRC, for his guidance and his editing skills and the staff of the DRC for their administrative support.

They are also grateful for the contributions made by Caroline Hartnell and Paddy Ross of the Charities Aid Foundation.

Executive summary

Non-profit organizations in South Africa today

The non-profit sector represents a significant part of the South African economy, although there is a dearth of reliable statistics: estimates of the number of non-profit organizations (NPOs) in South Africa range from 45,000 to 80,000. These organizations are varied: NPO activities include welfare services provision, health services delivery, education, development, advocacy and sport. Half of the organizations that responded to the survey carried out by the Development Resources Centre for this publication stated that they were involved in 'community development'. One third of organizations indicated that 'education and training' was their primary activity.

The DRC survey findings suggest that the non-profit sector may employ approximately half a million people. It also indicates that NPOs tend to have more volunteers than paid employees (10–19 volunteers on average per organization).

South African NPOs have generally had access to a variety of funding sources, both local and foreign. Organizations involved in development work, many of which emerged in the 1980s, have been heavily dependent on foreign donations, primarily from Europe and the USA. NPOs also raise a significant amount of money from the local corporate sector.

The context in which non-profit organizations work

The South African economy is the biggest in Africa. It has undergone a period of growth over the last three years, and further growth is expected in 1997 (although possibly slightly less than the 3.1 per cent achieved in 1996).

Perhaps the biggest threat to sustained economic growth is violence in the country. Although there has been a sharp decrease in political violence, violent crime has increased. The most feared and often most brutal forms of violence are associated with car-jacking.

Government attitudes to the non-profit sector have been ambivalent since the election in 1994. It was initially dismissive about the role that NPOs could play in strengthening democracy and contributing to development, but there are clear indications that government is now keen to develop partnerships with NPOs.

The Department of Welfare is responding to initiatives from the non-profit sector to change the current prohibitive legal framework to create a more favourable environment for NPOs to operate in. The Department also joined many NPOs in making a detailed submission to the government to reform the tax laws in order to encourage more individuals and companies to support NPO activities.

The needs of the sector

Following the transition to democracy, the non-profit sector in South Africa is facing severe problems. The most important of these is the drastic reduction in funding from outside South Africa. In the final apartheid years, huge sums poured into the South African non-profit sector from governments and other overseas sources, reflecting the desire of European governments and the USA to put pressure on the South African authorities. Now the funds have largely dried up or are being redirected to government institutions.

Further significant factors have been the loss of skilled leaders (to government and business) and a general lack of skills to meet the challenges posed by the new situation. The following have been identified as key needs if the non-profit sector is to play a full role in the development of the new South Africa:

- creation of sustainable funding mechanisms and the diversification of funding sources;
- training and building up skills and professionalism;
- overcoming divisions in the sector, particularly between NGOs and CBOs;

- changing methods of organization, to encourage those who will benefit to participate in the development process;
- consideration of new ways of measuring NPO activities which recognize both the values of NPOs and the requirements of donors and funders;
- greater clarity about the future roles of the non-profit sector.

Options for foreign donors

Although there is undoubtedly a need for more money throughout South Africa's non-profit sector, South African NPOs feel that it is vital that foreign donors should not simply donate cash; rather, they should deliver their support in a way that enhances the future development and independence of the sector. Supporting community foundations, endowing local organizations and supporting innovative pilot projects are three particularly valuable forms that foreign donor support could take.

South Africa: The people, the government and the economy

Since the inauguration of the Government of National Unity in 1994, the legislature has steadfastly shifted South African policies and practices in line with international norms. A strong emphasis on checks and balances has ensured that a culture of openness is interwoven into the fabric of this fledgling democracy. This emphasis has emerged partly from decades of close links between non-profit organizations and supportive international agencies, which in no small measure helped South Africans to counter the past regime's repressive policies.

South Africa has a vibrant non-profit sector that is keenly aware of the key role that non-profit organizations can play in fostering a lasting democratic society and in tackling the socio-economic legacy of apartheid – gross inequalities in incomes and in almost every other aspect of life.

The socio-economic legacy of apartheid

South Africa is often described as a mixture of first and third world economies. The Gross National Product (GNP) per capita figure in 1995 was US$3,100, making South Africa a middle-income country in World Bank terms. Notwithstanding this, if the average annual income of less than R800 (US$175) for black South Africans in rural areas is used as a measure, the country would be categorized among the poorest of the low-income countries.

Poverty is widespread as a consequence of deliberate apartheid policy, and South Africa has one of the most unequal distributions of income in the world. The average monthly income of white households was around R3,300 ($720) in 1990. During the same period, a typical black household (with a household size of ten people) was earning only 15 per cent of this amount. Furthermore, inequality appears to be increasing and big disparities of income are opening up among black South Africans. A 1994 study found that the wealthiest 10 per cent of South Africans accounted for 51 per cent of total income earned and the poorest 40 per cent accounted for only 4 per cent. In general, the poorest South Africans continue to be black, particularly those in rural areas and women.

The South African economy is dominated by six conglomerates that control 86 per cent of the shares listed on the Johannesburg Stock Exchange. Efforts are, however, being made to 'unbundle' these conglomerates, partially in order to broaden the share base of emerging black-owned companies.

Past spending on health, education, pensions, housing, infrastructure and other social services was highly discriminatory. The present government, non-profit organizations and the private sector thus face the enormous task of providing basic services for all South Africans. Adequate housing is a basic human need and is crucial to socio-economic development, the improvement of the quality of life and the prevention of disease.

In summing up the 'legacy' of apartheid, a small section of the country's population enjoy incomes, health and educational standards comparable to those of the most highly developed countries. The rest of the population, predominantly black, live in conditions which can be described as traditionally 'third world'.

The people

Population

The South African Institute of Race Relations (SAIRR) survey for 1995–96 puts South Africa's estimated population at between 41.9 million and 44.7 million. This would put the country beside countries such as Poland and Spain. The rate of population growth between 1990 and 1995 was estimated at 2.3 per cent a year – a rate of growth the SAIRR equates with that of the Philippines, Egypt and Lebanon.

Because of ineffective census procedures, some organizations such as the Centre for Development and Enterprise are quoted in the SAIRR survey as suggesting that South Africa's rate of population growth has been overestimated.

No accurate figures are available for the numbers of people migrating to South Africa, but undoubtedly substantial numbers are coming from other African countries, Asia and, to a lesser extent, Eastern Europe – mainly illegally. The number of economically active emigrants from South Africa has reportedly increased by 134 per cent between 1992 and 1994. The net gain of 'legal' immigrants to South Africa in the period 1984–94 has been estimated at 230,000.

In terms of the latest statistics, 21 per cent of the population live in KwaZulu-Natal, 17 per cent in Gauteng, 16 per cent in the Eastern Cape, 13 per cent in the Northern Province, 9 per cent in the Western Cape, 8 per cent in the North-West Province, 7 per cent in the Free State, 7 per cent in Mpumalanga and 2 per cent in the Northern Cape. Thirty-eight per cent of the total population live in KwaZulu-Natal and Gauteng, the two most urbanized provinces.

Language

South Africa is a highly cosmopolitan society with a wealth of languages, traditions and cultures. There are 11 official languages, nine of which are based on the Nguni and Sotho languages (Zulu and Xhosa are

both Nguni languages); these are predominantly the mother tongues of the black African population, which makes up 75 per cent of the total population. The other two languages are English and Afrikaans, which are predominantly the mother tongues of the white population (around 13 per cent), although many black people, particularly those of mixed heritage (in 'apartheid speak' people of mixed heritage are termed 'coloured') have Afrikaans and English as their first languages. Throughout this report the term 'black' will be used to refer to black Africans, people of Indian ancestry and people of mixed heritage.

Religion

This 'rainbow nation', as South Africa's cosmopolitan society is described, is also evident in the varied religions. Christianity is the religion of the majority of the people in the country, but significant numbers are Jews, Muslims, Buddhists, Hindus, Ba'hais, animists or ancestor worshippers. The country is generally secular and is no longer officially described as a 'Christian' country. Religious tolerance is a hallmark of South African society; in some communities mosques and Catholic and Protestant churches are built side by side, separated only by simple fences.

The country's pride in this diversity should not, however, mask the marked social and economic disparities between the majority black population and the white population, as described above.

Urbanization

There are no reliable statistics available on the number of people living in rural and urban areas. The majority of South Africa's population still live in rural areas, largely in areas designated by the apartheid government as 'homelands'. The majority of the urbanized black population live in apartheid-designed dormitory townships on the outskirts of the major cities.

Since the lifting of apartheid influx control measures aimed at keeping the cities 'white', people are flooding into the major metropolitan areas, pushed by poverty and lack of opportunity. The metropolitan areas have been deliberately underdeveloped for decades on the grounds that black people belong in the homelands. This rather unique policy to stunt urbanization has now resulted in the mushrooming of informal (squatter) settlements and in cities ill prepared to deal with this and other problems of rapid urbanization.

The government

The 1994 elections

South Africa's first democratic elections took place in April 1994. The elections were the culmination of two years of negotiations on the future of the country involving all the major political parties, including the National Party, the Democratic Party and the Inkatha Freedom Party (IFP), and liberation movements such as the African National Congress (ANC) and the Pan-African Congress (PAC).

The negotiations yielded an agreement that a new government would be based on proportional representation; parties would gain seats in parliament and the cabinet based on levels of support from the electorate. In the run-up to the elections there was widespread fear of a civil war, primarily because of conflicts between supporters of the ANC and the IFP, and a lesser threat of armed rebellion against the transition to democracy by a small grouping of white right-wingers.

Although there was violence and horrible loss of life due to these conflicts in the months running up to the elections, the elections themselves went off successfully. This success can be attributed partly to the hundreds of non-profit organizations that seconded their staff to be involved in all aspects of managing the electoral process. The smooth elections signalled the beginning of a relatively harmonious political discourse between all the major political parties in government.

The Government of National Unity

The ANC won the national elections by an overwhelming majority, falling just short of the two-thirds majority that in terms of the interim constitution would have allowed it considerable decision-making powers in the process of negotiating and writing a new constitution for the country. The National Party did surprisingly well: they gained 22 per cent of the vote and became the second biggest party in parliament, with considerable representation in the cabinet. The IFP, with 5 per cent of the vote, also qualified for two seats in the cabinet. These three parties thus formed a coalition government that was termed the Government of National Unity (GNU).

The Democratic Party and the Pan-African Congress did badly in the national elections; their representation was thus limited to parliament as they did not qualify for cabinet seats. The same was true of other small parties such as the African Christian Democratic Party. The Afrikaner Volks Front (AVF), a party coalition of groupings for Afrikaner 'self-determination', did better than expected in the elections, winning more votes than both the Democratic Party and the Pan-African Congress.

The elections saw Nelson Mandela become president of the country and quickly establish himself as one of the world's leading statesmen. Thabo Mbeki of the ANC became the First Deputy President and F W De Klerk, the former president of apartheid South Africa, became the Second Deputy President.

Provincial elections were also held in 1994. The ANC won seven of these nine provincial elections; the National Party won the election in the Western Cape and the IFP was successful in KwaZulu-Natal.

Tensions within the Government of National Unity
Between 1994 and 1996 the GNU became increasingly fragile. The cordial nature of the deliberations between the three parties within the cabinet diminished as debates on the detail of a new constitution came to the fore. The IFP walked out of the Constitutional Assembly, unhappy with the proposed powers to be given to the provinces and with the fact that the ANC had allegedly reneged on an agreement to get international arbitration to resolve issues of disagreement related to the constitution-making process.

The National Party left the cabinet as the constitution-making process came to an end. De Klerk asserted that the decision to become the official opposition was a vote of confidence in the emerging democracy and a sign that the South African transition had indeed been successful. President Nelson Mandela echoed this, and it seems as if the international community concurred and generally lent its support to the move.

With the National Party leaving the GNU, the ANC has more leeway to implement its programmes without having to negotiate with another major party. The IFP remains in the GNU but its ability to influence cabinet decisions is much less than was the case with the National Party.

The future 'after Nelson Mandela'
In recent months there has been much speculation about the future of the country 'after Nelson Mandela'. Mandela's image as perhaps the most respected head of state in the world has inextricably associated him with the 'South African miracle'. It is

thus understandable that many people, particularly outside the country, are uneasy about what will happen after his retirement. It should be borne in mind, however, that the South African transition was possible owing to the involvement of many people and institutions. There is sufficient leadership capacity in the current ruling party and within the main opposition parties to ensure that South Africa continues to steer itself successfully through the difficult years ahead.

The most likely successor, Thabo Mbeki, the vice-president, is probably more involved in the details of government than Mandela. Though Mbeki lacks the charisma of Mandela, arguably South Africa is fortunate in having a political successor of such calibre; to quote the *Financial Times*, 'he seems self-confident, widely read, possessed of a deep sense of the history of his country'.

National and provincial government powers
South Africa has a de facto federal system of government. In addition to the national parliament and cabinet, there are nine provincial governments, each headed by a provincial premier who presides over a Provincial Executive Committee (comparable to a provincial 'cabinet') and provincial legislatures. Although there are tensions relating to the division of power between national and provincial government, the provincial governments do have sufficient powers to ensure a level of independent decision-making.

The extent of provincial powers is still being debated. The Constitutional Court – the body responsible for ratifying the constitution and through which amendments to the constitution can be sought – recently decided not to adopt the constitution put forward to it by the Multi-party Constitutional Committee in Parliament on the grounds that the proposed constitution did not give the provincial governments sufficient power and autonomy. On the other hand, the Court also rejected the provincial constitution of the province of KwaZulu-Natal, which has a government headed by the IFP, on the grounds that the powers given to the provinces would then be tantamount to secession from the South African state.

The local government elections
The local government elections were held in November 1995. They followed the general pattern of the national elections, with the ANC doing extremely well throughout the country but coming second to the

IFP in KwaZulu-Natal and the National Party in the Western Cape.

The induction of the first representative local government in the country's history constituted the final element that was seen to be necessary for effective government action to provide for people's basic needs and implement the programmes outlined in the government's Reconstruction and Development Programme. Local governments will be responsible for drawing up development plans in partnership with organizations and individuals from local communities. The implication of this is that development NPOs will have a significant role to play in ensuring that local delivery of goods and services takes place effectively.

Government openness and transparency

The new South African government has committed itself to open and transparent government. An Open Democracy Bill is being debated in parliament; this would allow for a free flow of information between government and the public and enshrine the principles of administrative justice and the right to information that are part of the country's Bill of Rights.

There are debates as to whether the right to information should include prescribing disclosure procedures for the corporate sector and whether this would conflict with the right to privacy enjoyed by both individuals and corporations under the South African constitution and Bill of Rights.

The economy

South Africa has the largest and most sophisticated market economy on the African continent. The country represents only 3 per cent of the continent's surface area, yet it accounts for 40 per cent of all industrial output, 25 per cent of gross domestic product, more than half of generated electricity and 45 per cent of mineral production. About 75 per cent of South Africa's economic activity takes place in the country's four main metropolitan areas:

- the greater metropolitan area surrounding Johannesburg and Pretoria in Gauteng;
- the Durban/Pinetown area in KwaZulu-Natal;
- the Cape Peninsula in the Western Cape;
- the Port Elizabeth/Uitenhage area in the Eastern Cape.

The geographical clustering of the main areas of activity in the urban areas of what used to be termed 'white South Africa' is symptomatic of the general structural weakness of the economy. South Africa has a dual economy: a sophisticated industrial economy benefits a small proportion of the middle-class and upper-class urban population while an underdeveloped economy with high levels of unemployment afflicts the majority of the people in the country, particularly those living in the rural areas and former homeland areas.

The new government thus takes over an economy with serious structural weaknesses, which is also highly dependent on a changeable international environment and characterized by an uncompetitive industrial sector, a worn capital stock and high levels of unemployment.

Economic growth

The economy has undergone a period of growth over the last three years. In 1995 real economic growth was 3.3 per cent; this is the highest level since 1988, when the economy grew by 4.2 per cent. All sectors of the economy experienced growth in 1995 with the exception of agriculture and mining, which dropped by 14.9 per cent and 3.6 per cent respectively. In 1996 the economy grew by 3.1 per cent; this growth was primarily due to a strong rebound by the agricultural sector.

Government officials and economists forecast a similar or perhaps slightly lower figure for 1997, reflecting the likelihood of a tough budget and strict limits on government expenditure. This year, however, growth is expected to come from manufacturing, financial services and mining, which should help to boost the trade surplus (US$2.5 billion in 1966) and reduce the current account deficit. The longer-term outlook is reasonably favourable – the South African Economic Review forecasts real growth in 1998 of 3.5 per cent. However, prospects are still far from rosy and current growth rates are generally expected to be insufficient. The government has stated that unless the economy expands by at least 6 per cent a year, there can be little improvement in the country's severe unemployment problems.

The government has not yet made substantial changes to the market-based economy and it is unlikely that it will do so. It is committed to implementing its Reconstruction and Development Programme (RDP) with a view to providing opportunities and facilities for previously oppressed communities. The prime goal of the RDP is to enable historically disadvantaged communities to share equitably in the resources of the country and the fruits of its economic activity.

Many non-profit organizations active in development work had expected greater direct involvement in the economy by government in order to achieve some of the goals set out in the RDP. With the adoption of the Growth, Employment and Redistribution Strategy (GEARS – also known as the Macro-Economic Strategy), however, there is a more marked trend towards deregulation as the government tries to make South Africa more attractive to foreign investors and to ensure that the country is able to enter the global economy.

GEARS is seen by South African trade unions as contrary to the stated goals of the RDP. The key concern for trade unionists is that the new economic plan is largely modelled on plans followed by Western European countries over the last decade. The new economic plan should lead to growth, but there is a concern that as in many European countries it will be 'jobless growth'. An economic plan that stifled job creation in a country with very high levels of unemployment would indeed be a cause for concern.

Unemployment

According to the latest statistics (October 1994), approximately 33 per cent of the economically active population are unemployed, with unemployment among the black population running at 41 per cent. These figures correspond with recent poverty indicators. The Human Sciences Research Council household survey suggests that approximately 55 per cent of rural black households and 42 per cent of urban black households live in poverty. This compares with approximately 4 per cent of urban white households and 2.6 per cent of rural white households.

These statistics are based on the assumption that the poverty line for an urban household with two adults and three children is R840 per month (approximately US$185), with a figure of R740 ($160) for a rural household of the same size.

Crime and violence

Politically motivated violence

Violence has been a part of South African society for the past 40 years. The apartheid years were characterized by state and institutional violence, with the police and the army virtually terrorizing black communities. Recent revelations at the Truth and Reconciliation hearings on human rights abuses, both by the apartheid government and by the liberation movements, have unveiled the extent of state-sponsored violence. The state through its covert units fuelled political violence between supporters of the Inkatha Freedom Party (IFP) and the African National Congress (ANC). The result was tens of thousands of deaths, primarily in the KwaZulu-Natal area. As the people living in this area are predominantly Zulu-speaking, the myth propagated by the previous government that the violence was ethnic and largely a result of tensions between a Xhosa-speaking ANC movement and a Zulu-speaking Inkatha movement was exposed.

Although tensions in KwaZulu-Natal are still high, recent joint peace rallies addressed by the leaders of both the ANC and the IFP are beginning to yield results. This was most evident in the celebrations in honour of the nineteenth-century Zulu monarch, Shaka, where Zulu leaders of both parties addressed thousands of Zulu-speaking people. The theme of the rallies was the need to reduce the politically motivated killings among people living in the province.

Violent crime

Despite the general decrease in politically motivated violence, violent crime has increased. Although the perception that violent crime is a post-apartheid phenomenon is false, the nature of the violence is indeed disturbing. The most common and often most brutal forms of violence are associated with car-jackings. In the Gauteng region, 75 per cent of these take place in the predominantly black townships. Even more disturbing is the increased brazenness of gangs in the townships and of the organized syndicates that are at the heart of most crime such as car-jacking and drug dealing.

The effect of these violent crimes is the emergence of a siege mentality among South Africans, with many people afraid to leave their homes. The call for the death penalty to be reinstated has been deafening, and most members of the public feel that it would result in a lowering of the crime rate. Others feel that the only answer to the rampant criminality is to build the capacity of the police force and the justice system.

Significant progress has already been made with regard to enabling the justice system to deal effectively with organized crime. The Parliamentary Justice Committee has started drafting three pieces of legislation: the Proceeds of Crime Bill, which will empower the courts to confiscate the proceeds of criminal activities; the International Co-operation in Criminal Matters Bill, which will allow the courts to obtain help in obtaining evidence; and the Extradition Amendment Bill, which should make it easier to extradite suspects.

Crime prevention ultimately depends on reducing levels of unemployment and poverty and introducing a societal safety net for those who are poor and most likely to resort to crime for basic survival. Investment in social welfare would thus be more beneficial in the long term than building more gaols for people pushed out of the formal economy.

The non-profit sector in South Africa today

There are no reliable figures on the South African non-profit sector as a whole. This section outlines the basic facts in so far as they are documented. It also describes the different types of non-profit organization; the main sources of funding, foreign and domestic; the legal and fiscal framework within which the sector operates; and public and governmental attitudes towards the sector.

Basic facts about the sector

The number of non-profit organizations

It is extremely difficult to determine accurately the number of NPOs in South Africa because there is no current mechanism for collecting data on the sector. In 1994 the Development Resources Centre (DRC) and the South African Institute of Fundraising estimated that there were approximately 54,000 NPOs active in the country. Although this figure is still widely quoted, other estimates ranging from 45,000 to 80,000 organizations are also current.

Total money going to the sector

In 1993 the DRC estimated that almost R10 billion (US$2.2 billion) per year circulated through the sector. The estimates drew on figures compiled by a private marketing institution, Business Management Information. If the figures were reliable, then in 1993 the total amount of funding for South Africa's non-profit sector represented 4.7 per cent of GNP.

In 1996 a further survey was undertaken by the DRC in partnership with the Charities Aid Foundation in the UK. Questionnaires were sent to a random sample of 1,000 organizations, but only 108 responded – a response rate of 10 per cent. The respondents were probably not fully representative of the sector as a whole, in that, for example, 10 per cent reported very large total incomes of between R3 million and R13 million for the period 1994–95.

Given that many NPOs have experienced a funding shortage since the transition to democracy, owing to funds from bilateral and mainly European sources being diverted to the government, the survey findings relating to recent changes in income were also surprising. Forty-two per cent of respondents indicated that they had experienced an increase in income over the last two years, while only a third (34 per cent) reported a decrease. Twenty-four per cent of respondents indicated that their income had remained steady for the period 1994–95.

These results suggest that many organizations have managed to diversify their sources of funding significantly. Thirty-seven organizations out of 108 none the less indicated varying degrees of financial difficulties, and it seems almost certain, from other evidence, that total funding of the sector has in fact fallen since 1993.

Number of paid employees

The Community Agency for Social Enquiry, the organization that analysed the DRC's 1996 survey on NPOs, identified three categories of organization – small, medium and large – on the basis of numbers of staff members employed. Small organizations were defined as those that employ between 1 and 9 staff members, excluding volunteers, medium organizations employ 10–19 staff members, and large organizations employ over 20 staff members. Thirty-seven per cent of respondents were in the 'small' category, 23 per cent were 'medium' organizations and 40 per cent were 'large'. On the assumption (from these figures and the income data) that respondents were weighted towards larger NPOs, the overall average number of employees is probably around 15, or possibly fewer. In any event the sector employs a considerable number of people – at least 500,000 and perhaps more.

These figures are rather lower than those obtained in 1993, when the DRC analysed the staff statistics of 250 development organizations, using forms supplied to the Prodder Directory. (Prodder stands for the Programme for Development Research, a body that collects and disseminates information on all aspects of South African development.) Although the reported figures varied from 1 to 500, the average number of employees was found to be 34.

Type of staff employed

In the DRC's 1996 survey, respondents were asked to categorize their employees as 'professional', 'executive' or 'support'. Although professional staff made up the highest proportion in all organizations, this proportion increased significantly in larger organizations; the proportion of executive and support staff was roughly the same for small and medium organizations. Although definitions are not very precise, apparently it is the number of professional staff that increases as organizations get larger.

SIZE OF ORGANIZATION	TYPE OF STAFF		
	PROFESSIONAL	EXECUTIVE	SUPPORT
Small	45	21	34
Medium	41	22	36
Large	73	7	19

Number of volunteers

The 1996 survey indicated that 41 per cent of responding organizations had 1 to 9 volunteers; a further 41 per cent reported that they had more than 20 volunteers; 17 per cent reported that they had between 10 and 19 volunteers.

The DRC's 1993 survey indicated that some organizations had a very large number of volunteers. In 1993 the National Cancer Association reported that they had 7,000 volunteers, the St John's Ambulance Service reported that they had 6,000, the South African Red Cross reported 2,500, Youth for Christ reported 500, and AIESEC (Association Internationale des Sciences Economiques et Commerciales) reported 450.

Main areas of activity

Non-profit organizations are involved in a very wide spectrum of activities ranging from social welfare to assisting emerging entrepreneurs. The most frequently mentioned primary stated mission or aim of the organizations that responded to the 1996 DRC survey was 'community development'. This was mentioned by half of the respondents. This included generally promoting the enrichment and empowerment of the community, particularly formerly oppressed communities. 'Education and training' was cited by a third of respondents, while rural development was the stated primary mission of 14 per cent.

The most often mentioned primary activity was 'education' (46 per cent). This ranged widely from youth development to adult education to education on environmental issues. ' Capacity-building' projects were reported by less than half of all respondents (44 per cent). Job creation (including small and medium enterprise development) was the primary activity of just over a quarter of respondents (27 per cent).

Other areas in which NPOs are involved include urban development, housing and primary health care. There are also information-providing organizations such as the South African NGO Network (SANGONet), which provides e-mail and Internet services for NPOs and human rights advocacy.

Different types of non-profit organization

Venerable, emergency and transition NPOs

The DRC research indicates that NPOs generally emerged in three distinct phases. NPOs have thus been classified as 'venerable' or 'long-established', 'emergency' and 'transition'.

Venerable NPOs

Forty-five per cent of the organizations surveyed by the DRC in 1996 were founded in the period 1900–85. These 'venerable' organizations were primarily welfare-oriented and tended to have links with the formal welfare services provided by government.

Because of their association with the state, these organizations were generally mistrusted by many of the black communities, but their importance should not be underplayed. 'Traditional' charitable organizations play a very important role in providing basic-needs services to many communities. This role has become more focused as the welfare organizations are starting to engage more with other NPOs.

This period also saw the emergence of organizations such as the South African Committee for Higher Education and the Wilgerspruit Fellowship Trust, possibly two of the oldest 'development' organizations.

Emergency NPOs

'Emergency' organizations are those which were founded between 1986 and 1990 during the state of emergency declared by the apartheid government.

The Community Chest of the Western Cape

During 1995, 20 Community Chests in South Africa distributed R22.6 million to 732 health, welfare, educational and community-based development projects throughout the country, existing under the umbrella of the United Way of Southern Africa (UWSA). The UWSA acts as a national resource and information centre, and as a lobbyist and official representative of the Community Chest movement at both national and international levels. As one of the most efficient and cost-effective service deliverers, the UWSA is a major player in the country's reconstruction and development process.

The Community Chest of the Western Cape is the oldest and largest of South Africa's Community Chests, established in 1928 as a project of the Cape Town Rotary Club. It raises funds and distributes them to serve the welfare and social development needs of the community. It distributes some R10 million annually, supporting more than 300 welfare bodies (and in turn more than 1.5 million underprivileged people) in the Western Cape. In the face of government subsidy cuts, these funds allow welfare organizations to continue to deliver vital services to the community.

Beneficiaries cover a wide spectrum of human need, but programmes focus on family and child welfare services, services for physically and mentally handicapped people, and rehabilitation and health care support. The Community Chest carefully

evaluates the credentials and financial statements of all its beneficiaries, and then monitors the financial statements of organizations on an ongoing basis to ensure that funds are properly utilized.

Investments are the main source of income, providing over a quarter of total funds. Innovative scratchcards, the first introduced by a fundraising organization in South Africa, are the next most important method of income generation. A variety of cards are available from post offices and Community Chest kiosks, the catch-phrase being that 'Everybody wins with the lucky red feather' – the logo of the Community Chest.

The Community Chest is also widely supported by a 'Give-as-you-Earn' staff payroll deduction programme. Staff of more than 600 companies contribute as little as 50 cents per week, providing over 10 per cent of total fundraising income.

In 1989 the Community Chest acknowledged the need to establish a collective identity to promote the development of potential and existing Chests. This led to the registration of the UWSA (initially known as the United Community Chests of Southern Africa) in 1990. UWSA's sole source of funding is from the Independent Development Trust (IDT).

Contact Amelia Jones, Borwick House, PO Box 3836, 82 Bree Street, Cape Town. *Tel* +27 21 24 3344 *Fax* +27 21 24 7387 *Web address* http://www.cia.co.za/cchest

Twenty-seven per cent of the organizations surveyed by the DRC were founded during this period. These organizations are described by many as 'struggle organizations' because of the political nature of their activities. Advice offices, providing legal and other services, grew rapidly during this period. Civic organizations, set up to represent people's interests to the local black authorities in townships, also experienced unprecedented growth.

Many of these emergency organizations are finding it difficult to change their focus from being actively involved in fighting the apartheid government to carrying out development work and other activities needed in the post-apartheid era. This difficulty is compounded by the fact that many organizations founded during this period are finding that 'solidarity' funds from the European and US governments are being cut back.

Transition organizations

Twenty-eight per cent of the organizations surveyed by the DRC were founded between 1991 and 1995. The activities of these organizations tend to be related to policy work that will strengthen democracy and facilitate development. Organizations such as the DRC and more recently the Centre for Development and Enterprise, a policy think-tank on issues relating to urban development, are typical transition organizations.

NGOs and CBOs

The South African non-profit sector is also characterized by a distinction between what are termed non-governmental organizations (NGOs) and community-based organizations (CBOs). Although much of this distinction is about terminology, there are real differences between the two types of NPO.

'NGOs' tend to be urban-based organizations that have access to substantial funds and generally have skilled staff. In the past, they were generally led by predominantly white males. Many NGOs raised funds as intermediaries set up to 'build the capacity' of CBOs.

'CBOs' are small organizations with very little access to skills or funding. They tend to be located in rural and urban townships and are generally run by people living in the townships. Many CBOs are unhappy with the unequal access to funding between NGOs and CBOs and are actively campaigning for donors not to give funds to intermediaries but to channel funds directly to them.

In many areas, however, the distinction between an NGO and a CBO is difficult to make. There are organizations that have similar skill levels and equal access to funding and generally do the same type of work yet one is called an NGO and the other a CBO. Notwithstanding the very real differences, the term CBO has become a 'politically correct' term, and some new organizations call themselves CBOs in the hope that this will attract more donor funds.

On the whole the distinctions between NGOs and CBOs are a product of South Africa's history and much needs to be done to ensure that CBOs develop the infrastructure and skills to enable them to operate more effectively. Moreover, divisions or bad feelings between these different types of NPO may weaken the sector's ability to work together on issues of common concern.

Direct service providers

The bulk of NPOs active in South Africa are direct service providers either to a particular community or to a particular constituency. Direct service-providing organizations act primarily at grass-roots level and are quite diverse in terms of size, scope and income.

A number of international relief agencies have worked in South Africa but their activities have tended to reflect not only the economic environment

Alexandra Health Centre

The Alexandra Health Centre is a small but none the less important direct service provider. It provides a clinic service, including:

- an emergency unit which provides a 24-hour service;
- adult and paediatric outpatient departments which offer services from Monday to Friday;
- outreach services including satellite clinics.

The Alexandra Health Centre operates in Alexandra township north of Johannesburg. This is one of the most densely populated townships in Gauteng province and is characterized by high rates of unemployment and crime and a decaying infrastructure owing to a systematic lack of public and private service delivery during the last 40 years. There are enormous health problems in the area, and the Alexandra Health Centre is almost the only provider of health care.

Contact Nomvuyo Molefe, PO Box 175, Bergvlei 2012. *Tel* +27 11 440 1231 *Fax* +27 11 887 9007

Oxfam (UK and Ireland)

Oxfam UKI has worked in South Africa since 1956. It has focused funding on community-based anti-poverty programmes, supporting land reform and the rights of groups such as farm workers, labour tenants and women. Gender equality is promoted throughout the programme, with a specific focus on the violation of women's human rights, especially violence against women.

Reduced funding and new opportunities have forced a review of Oxfam UKI's approach. Other members of Oxfam International fund similar programmes in South Africa, and different Oxfams will now lead in particular sectors in South Africa. Oxfam UKI will concentrate on rural development, particularly in KwaZulu-Natal, Eastern Cape and Northern Province. This will include funding local development organizations and providing other support, drawing upon Oxfam UKI's experience and expertise elsewhere. It will focus on promoting rural livelihoods, while recognizing that it will not be possible to reduce poverty unless communities fragmented by violence are reconstructed (especially in KwaZulu-Natal) and people are enabled to put their hard-earned rights into practice.

Campaigning for change has always been part of Oxfam UKI's work in South Africa and the surrounding area. Under apartheid this included campaigns against forced removals and detentions under emergency laws, and working with farm and domestic workers. Campaigns launched in the UK included the 'Free Frontline Africa' campaign, which looked at obstacles to development in southern Africa and the impact of apartheid in South Africa. Aspects of this campaign were criticized by the Charity Commission in 1991, which argued that the campaign contravened UK restrictions on political involvement by charities. The controversy attracted widespread publicity in the UK – and the Commission has since revised its guidelines on charity campaigning.

Contact Nigel Taylor, PO Box 31009, Braamfontein 2017. *Tel* +27 11 339 2560/81 *Fax* +27 11 339 2740 *E-mail* oxfam@praxis.co.za

and problems but also the political situation in apartheid South Africa. Two examples of major UK charities with operations in South Africa are Save the Children Fund, which is established as an independent South African organization

Operation Hunger

Operation Hunger is a direct service provider but is none the less one of the biggest NPOs in the country. It is dedicated to alleviating malnutrition and poverty. Since it was founded in 1980, Operation Hunger has assisted hundreds of thousands of South Africans facing hunger owing to poverty, drought and the policies of apartheid.

From 1980 to 1994, Operation Hunger emphasized broad-based feeding programmes. But in 1994 the organization conducted a thorough internal review that reconsidered its role in post-apartheid South Africa. One outcome was that Operation Hunger resolved to focus its work in order to address the problems of malnutrition in a more comprehensive and sustainable manner.

The result is a development approach that targets the underlying causes of malnutrition by integrating water supply, health education, targeted feeding, environmental sanitation and food production (both for consumption and for income generation). Operation Hunger 'tested' this development approach at pilot sites throughout South Africa during 1995–96.

Operation Hunger receives funds from overseas donors, local government, corporations, trusts and foundations, and individual donors. It has seven regional offices, with a national head office in Johannesburg.

Contact P Davids, PO Box 32257, Braamfontein 2017. *Tel* +27 11 403 6750 *Fax* +27 11 403 1386

(in Johannesburg, Durban and Cape Town), and Oxfam, the UK's largest famine and disaster relief charity. Oxfam's focus in South Africa is rather different from the way it works in most other parts of the world.

Service organizations

There are a number of NPOs, normally termed service organizations, which work with grass-roots organizations active in different fields. Many do not themselves provide services, but work with direct service delivery organizations; others serve as networks for direct service providers. Most are involved in policy and advocacy work around specific issues. The National Progressive Primary Health Care Network is typical of such organizations.

National Progressive Primary Health Care Network (NPPHCN)

The NPPHCN promotes primary health care through campaigning for public policies that will result in better health care for South Africa's poor and marginalized communities. A number of organizations working on a range of health issues are affiliated to the NPPHCN and in fact 'drive' its advocacy activities.

NPPHCN promotes community involvement in health development with a special focus on the involvement of women in health programmes. It also conducts health education programmes for vulnerable groups such as children and disabled people. It provides

consultancy services and skills development workshops and training to primary health care organizations in the following areas:

- project development;
- fundraising;
- management;
- advocacy;
- training and participatory research methodologies.

Address PO Box 32095, Braamfontein 2017.
Tel +27 11 403 4647 *Fax* +27 11 403 1832
E-mail PPHCNJHB@wn.apc.org

Resource organizations and networks and agencies that support the sector

There are a number of organizations that are involved in activities that serve to strengthen the non-profit sector as a whole. These organizations provide information and consultancy services, carry out policy research work, campaign for public policies, and encourage private and community activities, including philanthropic giving, which strengthen the work of NPOs. Many of these 'tertiary' level organizations are also referred to as civil society resource organizations.

Development Resources Centre (DRC)

The DRC was set up in 1992 when South Africa's transition to democracy was just beginning. It upholds the view that a vibrant, independent development sector is central to creating and sustaining a just and equitable society. Its work is thus geared towards strengthening the sector. In doing this the DRC develops tools and techniques that enhance the sector's ability to test, challenge and advance existing practices and ways of thinking about development.

The DRC campaigns for innovative policies and development practices that will ensure optimal conditions for successful social development. The organization has spearheaded initiatives to change the legal and tax framework to enable NPOs to operate more effectively.

The DRC also provides access to appropriate training, through collaboration with educational institutions,

for the staff of NPOs involved in development work and facilitates participatory learning events. Its Information Centre provides development NPOs with resources such as funding contacts and criteria, training courses and materials, model constitutions and advice on legal issues pertaining to NPOs.

The Consultancy Service is involved in organizational development activities aimed at improving the effectiveness and efficiency of NPOs. The DRC also encourages the use of social auditing techniques to make NPOs more aware of the impact they have, both positive and negative, on the communities with which they work.

Contact Gavin Andersson, PO Box 6079, Johannesburg 2000. *Tel* +27 11 838 7504
Fax +27 11 838 6310 *E-mail* DRC@wn.apc.org

Where do non-profit organizations get their funding?

Direct foreign government support

South Africa's development NPOs have traditionally been heavily dependent on foreign donations. In the final years of apartheid, NPOs, particularly those which were actively anti-apartheid (which covered a wide range of organizations), were given support amounting to hundreds of millions of dollars. This was one of the ways in which European governments and the USA could put pressure on the South African authorities. Moreover, to quote from the latest *Development Update* published in 1996 by Interfund, a funding consortium established in South Africa since 1986: 'These funds were relatively easily accessed by the voluntary sector and were disbursed with a minimum of controls. As a consequence, voluntary sector organizations became overly dependent on funding from the north.'

With the advent of democracy, bilateral aid patterns are normalizing. There has been a shift away from direct relationships between foreign governments and South African development NPOs to relationships between governments. This has not necessarily resulted in less 'cash flow' overall but the government is definitely receiving aid previously channelled to NPOs.

The reduction in funding has affected not only organizations whose function was to monitor government activities or actively campaign against apartheid (such as the Black Sash, a long-established human rights organization with an international reputation) but many NPOs whose objectives are purely humanitarian.

No precise measurements of the decline in foreign funding are available but a June 1995 survey by the Independent Development Trust (a funding body set up by the South African government in 1990) provides quantitative evidence of the financial crisis faced by development organizations – NGOs and CBOs offering essential services to disadvantaged communities in the education, health, rural development, micro-enterprise and capacity-building fields.

This survey of 128 organizations showed that they had a total shortfall of R210 million (almost $46 million), two-thirds of their combined operating budgets in 1995–96. Even if funding promises were met, respondents still expected a shortfall, on average, of 34 per cent. This trend was confirmed by a later Interfund survey, also reported in the 1996 *Development Update*, with many of the organizations surveyed citing 'the precipitate withdrawal of the European Union and USAID – major funders in the past – as the source of funding constraints'.

Independent local channels of foreign support

European governments keen on supporting the non-profit sector both in their largely anti-apartheid activities and in their development activities tended to provide a large proportion of their funds through local 'conduit agencies'. The three best known of these agencies were the Kagiso Trust, the South African Catholic Bishops' Conference (SACBC) and the South African Council of Churches (SACC). These three agencies collectively channelled R436 million

Kagiso Trust

The Kagiso Trust was the major conduit for EU funds to NPOs in South Africa. In 1994 they distributed 100 million ecus (US$115 million) in new grants and in continuing support to existing projects. Since then EU income has fallen drastically and Kagiso has been able to fund very few new projects.

Foreseeing this development, Kagiso has set up Kagiso Trust Investments (KTI), a business venture, with separate directors and staff. The aims of KTI are the empowerment of the black community and the generation of funds for the Kagiso Trust. A range of enterprises have been established or are in the process of development. These include publishing, catering, motor distribution, radio stations and a major merchant banking venture (in conjunction with N M Rothschild, the UK banking group).

Kagiso is a smaller organization than in the past but it remains a key player in the South African non-profit sector. Its goal is self-sufficiency, through KTI building up a sufficient endowment to cover the Kagiso Trust's running costs, and preferably more. The Kagiso Trust would then distribute all the grants it receives from the EU and other sources and continue its role of strengthening the sector, concentrating particularly on CBOs and smaller organizations.

Contact Horst Kleinschmidt, PO Box 1878, Johannesburg 2000. *Tel* +27 11 403 7714 *Fax* +27 11 403 1940

from foreign sources to NPOs during 1991 (US$145 million at 1991 exchange rates).

There are no accurate figures available for funds currently channelled through these agencies but it is certain that the amounts are substantially less than they have been in the past. Funds coming to the Kagiso Trust from the European Union may have dropped by as much as 90 per cent.

There are also various smaller local organizations that raise foreign and domestic funds to support mainly black students with bursaries for secondary and tertiary education. They include the Equal Opportunities Foundation, the Educational Development Trust, the South African Institute of Race Relations and a number of others.

Private foreign funding sources

Private foreign funding comes mainly from corporations and foundations; the proportion provided by foreign private donors is very small. This has been the most stable source of funding for many development organizations. The distinctive feature of foreign funding is that it enables local organizations to embark on development and other activities that fall outside sometimes narrowly defined national priorities. This allows for vibrancy and innovation in the development field.

In recent years a number of foreign foundations have been active in supporting South African NPOs as a means of combating the legacy of apartheid and strengthening civil society. One of the first was Interfund. Established in 1986, this is a consortium of European and US NPOs which seeks to assist development organizations, primarily by funding educational and training projects. It has also published a series of authoritative reports, such as its 1996 briefing on development and the voluntary sector, *Development Update*.

Major US foundations with offices and significant programmes in South Africa include the Ford Foundation, the Charles Stewart Mott Foundation and the Open Society Foundation for South Africa (established in 1993 and funded, like other foundations in many countries in Eastern and Central Europe, by George Soros). In recent years Ford and Mott have put particular emphasis on strengthening the non-profit sector; they are both prepared to fund intermediary bodies and are concerned to support the sector's infrastructure.

Most foreign funders regard sustainability as a key issue when making decisions on funding proposals. Organizations have to demonstrate that they are

The Transitional National Development Trust (TNDT)

The TDNT was set up by the South African government in collaboration with the Kagiso Trust and the Independent Development Trust (IDT). The aim was to provide finance for effective NPOs that were in danger of closing owing to the hiatus in international donor funds. Seed money for the TNDT came from the European Union, with matching funds from the South African government.

The TNDT is a short-term structure that is to evolve into a statutory development finance body, the National Development Agency. It is currently administered by a board of trustees with 'representatives' of both NGOs and CBOs. Additional board members come from the IDT and the Kagiso Trust. The South African government has one representative on the board.

It is envisaged that the National Development Agency which will emerge from the TNDT will receive funds primarily from two sources. The first is South African government funds earmarked for development. In addition, bilateral aid intended to support the development activities of NPOs will be channelled to it. There is, however, still debate in government circles about the precise functions of the National Development Agency, following a report by the advisory committee for the new agency.

Many NPOs have stated that the National Development Agency should not become a magnet for private donor finance; they believe that private donor finance should involve a 'direct relationship' between NPO and donor as this contributes to a healthy partnership between them.

After briefly flirting with the idea in 1994, the government has stated that it has no plans to centralize all sources of donor finance for NPOs. Although it has asked donor agencies to fund organizations in accordance with government development priorities, it realizes that it would not be able to monitor this, except in relation to bilateral agreements.

Contact Paul Jackson, PO Box 31959, Braamfontein 2017. *Tel* +27 11 403 6650 *Fax* +27 11 403 2515

sustainable or moving towards this goal. This means that organizations applying for funding must have strategies for reducing their dependency on external sources. Given the brittle nature of the funding environment, it is widely felt that organizations attempting to raise funds from a variety of sources are more likely to continue operating and are in a sense 'a safe investment'.

South African government support

In the past South African government support for charitable organizations predominantly took the form of cash grants to registered 'welfare organizations'. This support was facilitated by the Department of Welfare, which would fund welfare organizations up to 70 per cent of their annual budgets. The organizations would then have to raise the remaining funds from other sources.

Welfare organizations are starting to be affected by much the same financial problems as other NPOs. The Department of Welfare has already expressed its intention of cutting its generous subsidies to these organizations. They will thus be compelled to raise a larger proportion of their funds from the South African public. Some organizations have risen to this challenge well. The South African Red Cross, for example, has embarked on some innovative fundraising practices such as collecting money from South African Airways passengers.

Corporate social investment

Corporate social investment (CSI) in South Africa is as diverse as the corporations themselves. The history of CSI began in the 1970s when there were a number of important developments. The first was a lecture by Meyer Feldberg, a professor of business at the University of Cape Town, in 1972. Feldberg exhorted business leaders to learn from their US counterparts and get involved in the communities in which they operated.

The next development was the setting up in 1973 of the Anglo American and De Beers Chairman's Fund, the largest corporate donor in South Africa. Anglo American initiated the formation of the Urban

Anglo American and De Beers Chairman's Fund

The Anglo American and De Beers Chairman's Fund is South Africa's largest corporate donor. It is the principal instrument through which Anglo American, De Beers and their associates direct their corporate social investment. In 1995 R53.5 million was spread over more than 1,100 separate grants, focusing on education and training projects.

The Chairman's Fund has a broad mandate to support any cause that is 'socially constructive'. As a result, its grant-making mirrors the changing patterns of socio-economic need, the diversity of private initiatives, and the non-profit sector itself. This broad base of funding, coupled with a country-wide coverage, gives the Fund the expertise and confidence to identify important cutting-edge projects from which donors with a more narrow focus might shy away.

The Chairman's Fund is structured in a way which enables it to support some very big projects which are of a sufficient scale to make a real impact on a particular problem. Each of these 'special projects' involves the Fund working interactively in partnership with the community group or organization involved. The Fund's early special projects were undertaken when the first cracks were appearing in apartheid, enabling the Fund to help bring into being many ground-breaking ventures in black, non-racial and technical education.

Traditionally, the special projects have been fixed and finite, allowing the Fund to move on to other ventures without creating long-term dependency. Increasingly, however, it has begun to support longer-term programmes, seeing them as effective instruments for innovation and for achieving a multiplier impact on development problems.

The capacity to undertake special projects sets the Chairman's Fund apart, although it is in the field of general donations that it makes its greatest overall impact. These one-off or short-term more modest grants are made to both new and established ventures, both to innovative projects and to conventional welfare work. The Fund has provided the platform from which many starter projects have grown to self-sufficiency, with the Fund continuing its support but its significance diminishing in relation to the project's growth. The Fund recognizes the importance of steady support to promising but struggling initiatives.

Contact M C Keeton, 44 Main Street, PO Box 61587, Marshalltown 2107. *Tel* +27 11 638 9111 *Fax* +27 11 638 4998

Foundation in 1976 as a private sector initiative to tackle development issues in the townships. Several foreign-based companies – mainly American – became involved in CSI during the turbulent 1970s.

In the early days most companies would have simply operated donations programmes concentrating particularly on the areas in which the companies' offices or plants were based, but gradually the scope of CSI was extended. A number of factors were influential in bringing about changes. These included:

- the 'Sullivan principles', formulated in 1977, which encouraged US-owned companies to take a more proactive role in CSI;

SAGA – The South African Grantmakers Association

Recently the benefits of cooperation have become apparent to some organizations. One result has been the establishment of the South African Grantmakers Association (SAGA). SAGA brings together local corporations and some northern NPO donor agencies. Its current membership consist of over 50 donors, including some individuals. A notable exception from SAGA's membership is the Anglo American and De Beers Chairman's Fund.

SAGA's members do not pool funds or attempt to forge common funding policies; the focus is rather on information-sharing and communication among donors. SAGA is also seeking to work with the NPO community (non-donor) in efforts to establish a funding and taxation environment that is more favourable to NPOs. SAGA's other activities include:

- fostering professionalism and training in grant-making;
- promoting local and regional grant-making institutions;
- supporting research and learning on issues related to grant-making;
- developing creative partnerships for development.

SAGA has thus heralded a significant move in the development of information for and about donor institutions. If partnered with information-based NPOs, it could provide an effective information service about donors to local NPOs.

Contact address PO Box 10499, Johannesburg 2000. *Tel* +27 11 403 1610 *Fax* +27 11 408 3998

- a greater willingness by companies to work together and share ideas (culminating in the setting up of JET in 1990 – see p 28);
- more publicity for CSI, conferences and seminars on the topic, and generally greater awareness on the part of companies;
- the influence of the Anglo American and De Beers Chairman's Fund, which has been prepared to fund a wide range of organizations, including many operating in black communities.

CSI is typically biased towards particular areas of activity. The bulk of expenditure has gone to activities such as education and training – largely because donations to organizations working in these fields are tax-deductible, which is not the case for most NPOs.

Since the growth spurt in the seventies, corporate donations have grown to the extent that companies are now the second largest contributor to development after government.

With direct foreign aid being reduced, many NPOs are looking to the corporate sector as the answer to their financial problems. This aim is unlikely to be realized, for several reasons. Many companies, particularly smaller ones, do not have CSI budgets. Even those that do have money for this purpose are reluctant to increase their expenditure and may be uneasy about funding organizations about which they have little information. Most NPOs do not have the relevant fundraising expertise and skills – and acquiring such knowledge is not easy (and may be costly for organizations with small resources).

Corporate donors in South Africa have been reluctant to cooperate with each other and to maximize resources. Many companies feel that if they collaborate with other companies they might lose 'market visibility'. This is indicative of the fact that for many companies CSI is part of a marketing and public relations exercise. In fact, until recently many companies' CSI activities were coordinated by their public relations divisions.

Corporate-created independent grant-making trusts

These grant-makers are distinct from CSI in that they are relatively independent from the companies that created them. They also tend to be more proactive in supporting development work. The Joint Education Trust is perhaps the biggest of these, with an initial investment of R500 million (US$109 million).

Joint Education Trust (JET)

JET was launched with a commitment of R500 million from 20 of South Africa's largest companies and the participation of ten CBOs representing a wide spectrum of those dispossessed by apartheid. The mission of the Trust was to:

- focus on the development of the poorest communities;
- improve the quality of education and the relationship between education and the world of work;
- show short-term results and contribute to the long-term restructuring of the education and training system.

JET is more a development agency than a funding agency. It enters into long-term contracts with the organizations it supports, and subject to review such contracts can be renewed annually. Sustainability is becoming very important to NPOs as a result of the funding crisis prevailing in South Africa. JET's approach is to encourage NPOs to charge fees for the services they provide and to align these services with government service provision strategies.

Given the importance of evaluation to the development process, JET encourages agencies and organizations that offer evaluation services to the sector. JET also offers NPOs information management services, encouraging NPOs to keep account of whom they work with, where they go for funding, and any other work-related activities, including critical research based on fieldwork.

JET will have disbursed all its initial funds by the end of 1998. It is now seeking to mobilize new sources of funds from government, foreign donors (such as the European Union) and the private sector.

Contact Hugh McLean, PO Box 178, Wits 2050. *Tel/Fax* +27 11 339 3212

Direct individual giving

Until recently there has been a general perception that the bulk of funding to NPOs in South Africa comes from individual sources. In 1993, based on figures supplied by the South African Institute of Fundraising (which deals mainly with 'welfare' organizations, which tend to get a large proportion of their funds from individual giving), the DRC estimated that the bulk of the sector's income was attributable to individual giving by members of the public; this included workplace giving and grants from private trust funds.

However, the organizations surveyed by the DRC in 1996 indicated that they received a small proportion of their funds through direct contributions from members of the public. These findings are similar to those of a June 1995 survey of 128 organizations by the Independent Development Trust to 'measure' the extent of the recent funding crisis.

There is no doubt that a significant proportion of registered welfare organizations do receive substantial amounts from members of the public. These welfare organizations, mainly involved with care for older people, children and handicapped people, family counselling and poverty relief, have traditionally been more adept than other NPOs at raising funds from individuals.

Many of these organizations could raise money effectively from individuals precisely because they could appeal to the white community where the bulk of their services were being rendered. This should not, however, detract from their achievement in developing and utilizing innovative fundraising practices. Nevertheless, the Department of Welfare has estimated that up to 70 per cent of these organizations' funding comes from government sources.

The legal framework

The legal framework within which South African NPOs currently operate is constituted by:

- the legal options for establishment of an NPO;
- the Fundraising Act, under which NPOs have to apply for authority to raise funds from the public.

The establishment, registration and administration of NPOs

Under current South African legislation, an NPO that wishes to set itself up and start operating can choose from three legal entities. It can set itself up as a trust, a voluntary association or a section 21 company.

Trusts

The objects of a trust, the power of the trustees, and the entire operational and management framework of the trust are governed exclusively by the provisions of the trust deed, and there is limited state regulation. The trust deed must be lodged at the office of the Master of the Supreme Court.

One problem with trusts is the lack of any significant statutory control, and the fact that they are not publicly accountable for the way they spend their money. This may mean that donors prefer to make donations to a company rather than a trust.

Section 21 companies
The incorporation, regulation and dissolution of a company is governed in minute detail by the comprehensive provisions of the Companies Act.

A section 21 company is a special form of company that is incorporated as an association not for gain. A section 21 company may make a profit but cannot distribute its income and assets in any manner whatsoever to its members. Income and assets must be utilized solely in the furtherance of the company's main object.

The disadvantage of a section 21 company is that the complex requirements and high setting-up costs make it an inappropriate legal form for many small grass-roots NPOs. In addition, many NPOs may need more freedom to choose how to structure themselves and run their organizations.

Voluntary associations
An NPO which wishes to establish itself without any state regulation at all can become a voluntary association. A voluntary association is governed by the common law and is created by agreement between three or more people. It need not have a written constitution, but an NPO setting itself up as a voluntary association would probably require a constitution to satisfy donors.

As long as certain legal requirements are complied with – including the requirement that there is no profit motive – the constitution can make provision for any arrangement that the NPO chooses.

The disadvantage of voluntary association status is that donors may require a legal form that imposes greater control, particularly when large amounts of money are at stake.

Difficulties with the present law
While the legal forms described above provide a number of options for NPOs to choose from, there are problems in respect of these, including:

Complexity The law applicable to NPOs wishing to register is extremely complex. There is a general lack of information in the NPO sector as to which legal forms are appropriate and how to set them up.

Undue reliance on experts Grass-roots NPOs with meagre resources should not need to rely on a small coterie of lawyers in order to get established. Information on the registration and administration of NPOs should be simplified and the need to rely on experts reduced.

State bureaucracy Registration of a company or a trust can involve difficulties and delays, particularly for smaller organizations.

The Fundraising Act
The core of the Fundraising Act – which is very much a product of the pre-apartheid environment – is contained in Section 2:

'No person shall collect contributions unless he is authorized thereto in terms of this Act and unless the collection takes place in accordance with the provisions of this Act.'

The definition of 'contribution' is wordy and complex, but in practice it includes all types of donation or gift. 'Collect' basically means to receive contributions from the public. The key question is therefore what 'the public' means in this context. This question has given rise to considerable doubt as far as contributions from *inside* South Africa are concerned.

The position with regard to overseas money is clear. Section 1(2) of the Act expressly provides that any contribution obtained from a person or organization outside the Republic is deemed to have been collected from the public inside the Republic. In other words, it is theoretically not possible to receive any 'contribution' from outside South Africa without a fundraising permit.

Fundraising authority is granted by the Director of Fundraising, who is appointed by the Ministry for Welfare and Social Development. Organizations which are regulated by other legislation are exempt, as are government-controlled institutions, churches, educational institutions and political parties.

Difficulties with the present law
Difficulties in obtaining a fundraising number The Director has a wide discretion to grant or refuse to grant authority to collect funds, commonly described as a 'fundraising number'. If the Director regards an applicant as non-political and within the traditional welfare field, such as early childhood education and health services, it is not difficult to obtain registration, although this is subject to the Director's wish to avoid 'overlapping and competition' between fundraising

organizations. If an organization is small and local, establishing that it is meeting a unique need is straightforward, but problems have often arisen for organizations supposedly in conflict or 'competition' with 'establishment' organizations.

A number of significant NPOs established to combat apartheid and its effects, or whose work has taken that direction, have avoided the Act. These organizations felt that there was no point in applying for a number: they believed that they had no prospect of obtaining one, and applying for one would merely have drawn unwanted official attention to the organization.

Complexity of regulations NPOs that have a fundraising number are required to make annual returns to the Director. Those that do not comply can have their number withdrawn. However, many NPOs are ignorant of the legal requirements and do not comply with all the complex regulations.

Failure to prevent fraudulent collecting and embezzlement In practice, the legislation has not prevented fraudulent collecting or embezzlement of funds. Even if a fundraising authority is withdrawn, an organization can carry on operating and raising funds.

The Act has increasingly fallen into disuse. Applying for fundraising permission is time-consuming and complicated, and many organizations conclude that it is more convenient simply to ignore the Act. The government is now committed to repealing the Act and replacing it with new regulatory legislation.

Improving the system for establishment and registration

It needs to be considered what legislation can do positively to assist the non-profit sector. It should establish easy registration procedures, create accessible information about registration, give information to NPOs on benefits available and enable registration to be quick and efficient.

The fundamental right that already exists in South African law which enables an NPO to set itself up and start operating should be left untampered with. An NPO should not be required to ask permission to use the existing legal options and begin its operation.

Nor should legislation curtail the activities of NPOs or constrain and hamper them on the assumption that they will violate the law. The law should operate punitively only after it has been broken or after the

NPO has failed to account in accordance with the laid down procedures.

Replacing the Fundraising Act

The starting point for any new legislation should be a recognition that the central issue should not be how funds are raised but how they are spent and accounted for. In other words, the primary concern should be not what methods organizations use to raise money but how they spend the money they have raised and how they account to donors for the money they have received.

The key function of legislative 'control' of fundraising organizations should be to provide machinery to ensure financial accountability and transparency of NPOs, and liability where there is no such accountability and transparency.

The tax position

The tax regime governing charitable giving in South Africa is relatively unfriendly to NPOs. The present taxation policies are summarized below.

Income tax exemptions for NPOs

NPOs have generally attempted to obtain income tax exemption under Section 10(1)(f) and 10(1)(fA) of the Income Tax Act. However, exemption applies only if an NPO can show that it is of an 'ecclesiastic, charitable or educational' nature and is of a 'public character'.

It has proved extremely difficult to bring a range of development institutions under the ambit of the section. For example, the Department of Revenue considers educational institutions to be only those which promote a definite course of study. It takes a similarly narrow view of charitable organizations, considering 'soup kitchens' and 'orphanages' to be charitable in purpose but not organizations concerned with uprooting poverty through helping communities to help themselves. This means that most development NPOs cannot obtain exemption.

Some NPOs experience further restriction because they are classified as 'funds' rather than 'institutions' and so fall under the more restrictive Section 10(1)(fA).

Funders in South Africa, both local and foreign, feel strongly that the existing law is affecting the level of giving. Many donors do not fund organizations that do not have tax-exempt status.

Tax deductions for donors for donations to NPOs

Section 18A of the Income Tax Act allows donors to deduct the amount of certain donations from their taxable income. This provides some encouragement to individuals and organizations to make donations. The problem with this section is that it applies only to 'educational funds, universities or colleges'. The majority of organizations involved in poverty relief, welfare and development activities are thus excluded from its provisions.

The South African tax regime also includes a positive disincentive for donations, in that donors must pay an additional tax on any donation above the following amounts:

- in the case of a company, 5 per cent of its taxable income for that year;
- in the case of any other taxpayer, R500 (US$109) or 2 per cent of taxable income, whichever is less.

Possibilities for change

Over the last two years, NPOs and others have been considering ways in which the legislative and tax regime might be made more favourable. This was the main topic of the 'NGO Week' conference held in Johannesburg in December 1996. The government, in particular the Department of Welfare, has been sympathetic. The Chief Director of Social Development at the Department wrote for the *Johannesburg Star* that the Department has been 'dependent on NGOs for much of its delivery . . . Next year (the) Department's NGO Directorate will be initiating legislation to create an environment more favourable to NGOs.'

Some of the ideas for change that are being considered are set out below.

Income tax exemptions for NPOs

Section 10(1)(f) applies to 'charitable, ecclesiastical or educational' institutions. The word 'charitable' could, however, include most development organizations within its ambit if interpreted broadly rather than narrowly. Such a redefinition would mean that the whole range of NPOs covered in this report would benefit from the exemptions.

It has also been suggested that NPOs should not automatically be denied tax exemption because they engage in trading activities. NPOs should still qualify for exemption if, first, trade is exercised in the actual carrying out of the primary purpose of the NPO or, second, the work in connection with the trade is mainly carried out by beneficiaries of the NPO.

Broadening the scope of deductions for donors

Giving by individuals could be significantly boosted if the maximum deduction for individuals was increased to 5 per cent of the individual's taxable income, to bring it into line with the limit for companies. More importantly, a strong case can be made for making all gifts to a broad range of NPOs, including development NPOs, tax-deductible.

Consumption taxes

VAT is a major expense for NPOs, since as in other countries they do not have 'input' VAT to offset against this. It has therefore been suggested that organizations that are involved in poverty relief activities should be zero-rated for VAT, while all other NPOs should receive a 25 per cent rebate.

Attitudes to the sector

Government

The government's attitude to the sector has been ambivalent over the last two years. After the elections in 1994 government veered towards dismissing NPOs and regarding them as superfluous in the new democratic order. This was perhaps because many newly elected politicians and civil servants were founders of the 'emergency' organizations that had been primarily involved in activities to usher in a new democracy and were now regarded as having fulfilled their missions. This dismissiveness of emergency organizations led to negative attitudes towards the sector generally.

Owing to advocacy work carried out by many organizations on the nature of the non-profit sector and its importance as a partner in development and democracy, government has begun to appreciate the contributions of the sector. Many government departments now regularly engage NPOs around policy issues and 'farm out' service delivery work to NPOs. The government is also keen to abolish laws restricting the work of NPOs and to introduce more enabling legislation. The Department of Welfare made a submission to the government-appointed Tax Commission arguing for tax benefits for NPOs.

The public

Much of the euphoria which followed the 1994 elections has now dissipated. South Africa's reconstruction effort has made slow progress and there has been a lack of coherent development organization in all sectors of society. There are many reasons for this. One of the most profound is an expectation that the state will 'deliver', which has tended to restrict popular initiative.

In economic terms it is impossible for the state acting alone to provide for social well-being. To meet the scale of need that exists in a society that has been systematically mismanaged and impoverished over generations requires financial resources well beyond the limits of government taxation. In political, cultural and spiritual terms, state programmes face even greater constraints. Yet South Africans, accustomed to a strong central state, and recognizing that the state is the most powerful social actor, have all too easily looked towards government as the sole initiator of development. (The business sector's position may be regarded as contradictory, for it appears to accord responsibility to the state for changing social conditions while simultaneously arguing for greater control by the market and privatization of state assets.)

The perception that only a strong state can 'deliver' what people need is matched by the perception by some members of the public that NPOs cannot make an impact on basic-needs delivery or welfare and other development programmes. These attitudes not only inhibit local initiative but also contribute to a reluctance by the public to contribute funds to NPO development programmes.

The needs of the non-profit sector

The non-profit sector is subject to some endemic constraints. Chief of these is the fact that it is principally a 'funded' sector, depending on grant finance from the corporate sector, private foundations or governments. This dependence makes it difficult to plan for the long term with any degree of confidence. A further issue is the fact that NPO personnel work for the poor but are seldom *of* the poor. This factor poses special challenges, as it does in most countries of Africa.

In addition, the non-profit sector in South Africa faces specific difficulties arising out of the circumstances of the end of apartheid and the transition to democracy. While the run-up to the elections of April 1994 saw the suspension or dilution of normal activity by many NPOs, the months immediately after the inauguration of the new Government of National Unity found the non-profit sector in disarray. Three factors in combination led many leading NPOs to become preoccupied with internal problems – and spectators in the broader political processes – to the detriment of their planned programmes: the loss of skilled leaders, the fall in foreign government funding and the lack of expertise to meet the new challenges.

Increased funding and sustainable funding mechanisms

Significant changes have occurred with regard to funding of the non-profit sector. Many foreign government agencies which funded NPOs for reasons of anti-apartheid solidarity now direct their resources towards the new government. As a result often unseasoned managers are having to focus on the need to harness meagre resources and try to cope with the new emphasis on cost recovery for services. Diversification of funding sources is crucial for NPOs if they are to survive.

Increased and continued solidarity between individual and private organizations outside South Africa and the local non-profit sector is welcomed. However, as a feasibility study undertaken by the DRC for the UK Charities Aid Foundation indicated, there is a need to develop institutions that will lay the basis for enduring financial sustainability for the non-profit sector in South Africa.

There is an obvious need for assistance to institutions that will encourage local and international corporate and individual giving. The need for a 'CAF-type organization', providing a range of financial services for donors and NPOs in South Africa, emerged clearly from the feasibility study.

Also related to NPO sustainability is the need for donors to contribute funds to organizations to establish endowments so that the cyclical dependence on donor funds is diminished. The establishment of community foundations would also provide a means of facilitating sustainable financing of community-building activities.

Leadership skills and new areas of expertise

With the end of apartheid an established layer of skilled leadership left the non-profit sector overnight to take up positions in national or provincial parliaments or the civil service, and even within the corporate sector. A new generation of leaders is struggling to build up its expertise, even as societal shifts require changes in organizational strategy and culture.

The expertise acquired by NPOs in the years of struggle may in any case be inadequate to meet the challenges of the new period. New roles are emerging for NPOs, and comprehensive strategic planning has become a prerequisite for organizational survival. The rigour of community-level business planning has replaced vague motivations as the starting point for development action. Participatory development methodologies (which emphasize that the people who will benefit from development must participate in the development process) require changes to programmes, internal structures and organizational processes. Advocacy has become an essential element in mobilization for action around broader social issues, including partnership with business and government.

New skills are needed if NPOs are to prosper – or indeed survive – in the new environment. Fundraising and money management are becoming an essential area of expertise for many more organizations. Political and campaigning NPOs are having to redefine their roles and redirect their activities.

So great has the scale of the challenge been for NPOs that they have in many cases become largely inactive, and a few have disappeared. A brief survey of organizational effectiveness, as South Africa embarks on an epoch of unprecedented community development effort, shows that there is a need to nurture and strengthen the competence of the non-profit sector. This applies to the emerging community-based development organizations (CBDOs) as much as to the established NGOs. However, the number of competent capacity-building organizations appears insignificant when viewed against the giant scale of need for their services.

Overcoming divisions in the sector

Bad practice in the non-profit sector in South Africa, from the late eighties until the inauguration of the new government, has left a legacy which hinders effective collaboration in development work. At the time of the elections, a rough sketch of the state of the sector would have included the following:

- an experience of small projects working in isolation, with limited ability to change social realities;
- an NGO sector which had portrayed itself as *intermediary* to community-based organizations (CBOs) but which had seldom empowered them, thus creating resentment on the part of the CBOs (proportional to the extent of their dependency);
- antipathy to the sector on the part of many civic organizations and community interest groups and some political actors;
- a donor fraternity which had become increasingly concerned about poor accounting and other unprofessional practice.

Of course there were exceptions to these broad trends: some hugely successful NGOs, a few vibrant CBOs and some productive development partnerships. And everywhere there was readiness for a new paradigm: a move towards small project funding, and away from the funding habit of donor to intermediary to grass-roots organization.

The months after the elections have, in many areas, seen the continuance of the 'split' between NGOs and CBOs. There is still a need to find mechanisms by which grass-roots organizations can access appropriate technical support. But the immediate history of the sector has resulted in hostility to 'intermediary' organizations, and many NGOs tend to be seen as falling into this category. Government, and several donor organizations, explicitly advocate a policy of sidestepping the intermediary organizations and instead providing resources for CBOs themselves to contract services either from NGOs or from private sector consultants.

Just as NGOs used to be idealized, CBOs are now starting to be idealized: this organizational form is always deemed accountable to the grass roots, and expressive of the real needs of the community. Such an attitude is based on two assumptions, neither of which is fully valid:

- first, that everywhere there are vibrant CBOs with the requisite capacity to screen organizations and individuals tendering for work, and to check the quality of delivery;

- second, that the 'development marketplace' will provide enough in contract fees to sustain technical support organizations and so ensure that there is a steady learning from experience and consequent improvement in quality.

Participation in development

Development forums and social compacts

The last year has seen the building of chains of representative organizations. *Development forums* have started to spring up around the country – bodies which bring together stakeholders within various communities to discuss needs and priorities and to form partnerships for development. These forums have the potential to weld together powerful local alliances in the interests of community development processes. They also have the potential to exclude all but the most powerful stakeholders and to become blocks to development, or the new intermediaries for development funding.

A similar observation can be made about many of the *social compacts* which are being formed. Social compacts are agreements between government organizations, private sector organizations, trade unions and NPOs to work together to develop economic and social strategies that would benefit the poor. They are thus agreements made between powerful stakeholders within a community, but the weak and poor are seldom able to articulate their viewpoints and participate meaningfully in the planning process.

However, a lesson repeated many times, in countries all around the world, is that development programmes tend to fail unless their processes and benefits are 'owned' by those who are their principal beneficiaries. There is no chance of sustainable programmes without the participation of those directly affected.

Many questions arise here:

- What kind of organizational forms are needed in a democratic society if a widespread and effective mobilization for development action is to be achieved?

- How will these organizations engage in participatory learning processes, and spread the lessons gained from their experience to others in society?

- How will the varied needs of diverse social actors find expression and satisfaction?

Catalysing the emergence of local-level development initiatives

One of the chief constraints on development in South Africa is the lack of local-level institutions which can take forward the development visions of communities. Genuinely local organizations could provide a means for expressing and actively addressing the varied and complex needs of society.

The newly emerging *popular development organizations*, where a team of professionals is directed by and accountable to its constituency, and so responsive to community needs and interests, may provide a blueprint for durable organizations which can address a range of issues. Once a community is able to understand the wider context within which it is organizing, can access resources and appropriate information, and has an organizing framework that enables it to learn systematically from its organizing experiences, it will be able to improve its well-being steadily.

The organizational forms which will emerge in the epoch ahead may serve another role, even while their main focus is on addressing felt needs. An ancillary result of the creation of local-level organizations is that individuals become motivated to act as citizens in all aspects of society rather than depending on state power and beneficence.

Measuring NPO activity

A widespread problem for donors, in all countries, is how to evaluate and measure NPOs and NPO activity. This partly reflects the fact that for much NPO activity, particularly in the development field, the *process* is almost as important to NPOs as the *end-product*.

The period ahead will see NPOs entering into contracts with government or with communities to perform certain tasks. NPOs thus enter the arena of trading organizations (the business sector); in competing in the marketplace they will have to demonstrate cost-effectiveness in delivering their products. The 'implicit contracts' of previous years are now being replaced by explicit contracts to deliver a definite product within a given period of time. The challenge for NPOs is to find mechanisms which embody their values and also meet the requirements of the marketplace. This may mean looking at the way the contract is drawn up.

To take a simple example, the case of digging a well. An NPO with this task would seek to consult the community, 'reveal' the need and then dig the well (in the manner which optimizes participatory learning); for a business consultant the objective is merely the end-product, the digging of the well (in a manner which realizes maximum profits). Exclusive focus on the product can result in a one-dimensional understanding of development, which may neglect many of the real needs of a community. In this example the NPO would strive to work in the way it judges to be most useful in the longer term, to build community self-reliance, and to ensure that the projects taken up are appropriate to people's concerns and satisfy real needs.

Demonstrating long-term success and measuring the effectiveness of an NPO's work means designing new tools. Measurement in terms of product and finance costs is insufficient to capture the complexity of the social interests involved, but the NPO has nevertheless to demonstrate to funders that it is efficient and provides good value. The need is for more transparency and better accountability to all stakeholders, including both funders and the people served by NPOs.

Defining the future roles of the non-profit sector

Much has been said about the potential roles of the non-profit sector. In some respects any attempt at definition could be said to be an artificial exercise, since the non-profit sector consists of thousands of organizations with widely divergent areas of work. There is nevertheless some value in people having a clearer idea of the role that the non-profit sector could play in developing the new South Africa. What follow are some suggestions about areas of work to which NPOs are particularly well suited.

Implementing innovatory schemes
A role often assumed by NPOs is that of testing a new technology or organizational methodology. Lessons from practice are then incorporated in forthcoming project design. Once it is clear that a particular

approach is viable, it may be possible to build social partnerships which allow the approach to be replicated widely.

Influencing policy
There is a role for the non-profit sector to play in generalizing from practical lessons and documented experience in order to propose changes to policy, procedure or technical instruments. This kind of work could range from the design of management systems in a huge presidential project through developing mechanisms for lodging land restitution cases to the proposing of a new law. Any work to improve the conditions for effective social action requires active involvement by NPOs in community organizations or participatory action research.

Mediation and partnership building
Being well placed to observe trends, opportunities, organizational strengths and resource flows allows NPOs to interact with community organizations, business, government and other civil society organizations to propose mutually beneficial partnerships. Effective mediation between diverse stakeholder interests is a valuable contribution to local-level development.

NPOs as extensions of government departments
A common vision for the non-profit sector, from the government perspective, is that NPOs should engage in government-designed programmes, thus extending the work of government departments. A number of schemes are proposed at present which envisage this kind of partnership.

The key issue here is the role NPOs take within such partnerships. They may work to enhance participatory planning processes, popular action and participatory learning. If they cannot do this, it is difficult to see what value is created by their involvement.

Providing commercial services
Some NPOs sell specific services outside the ambit of government programmes. Many of these organizations are exceptionally efficient; they are competitive with the private sector while at the same time facilitating community participation and skills acquisition.

Options for foreign donors

At the conference billed as 'NGO Week', held in December 1996 for the non-profit sector in South Africa, the role of foreign donors was discussed in depth. While there is a general need for funding, it was thought to be vital that donors should direct their support towards NPOs that are working for the long-term development of South Africa and the sustainability of the non-profit sector. This section outlines some of the areas of work that were identified as priority areas for donors to support.

Supporting community foundations

South African NPO delegates and spokespersons for numerous private donor agencies agreed that there was a need for donors to look at means to increase the ability of local NPOs to raise funds locally. Key to this was the idea that donors should support initiatives to build effective community foundations so that NPOs and other community organizations would have access to a stable source of funding. This type of support would include providing institutional support to NPOs working to establish new community foundations or to strengthen existing ones.

Equally important would be support for training the board and staff members of emerging community foundations. This should include providing funds for staff members to do extensive internships in successful community foundations outside South Africa. If community foundations are to be successful, it will be important for donors to contribute to their initial endowment, even if this is on the basis of matching funds provided by local donors.

Endowing local organizations

The funding crisis faced by many organizations arises partly from the fact that they have to raise and receive project funds on a year-to-year basis. This cycle of raising and spending funds constrains the abilities of NPOs to be innovative, and many tend to adapt their programmes to meet the changing needs and interests of donors. Perhaps the best contribution donors can make to sustainable funding mechanisms is to provide organizations that are active in areas that meet the strategic missions and values of donors with funds to establish investments and endowments. This would give organizations a steady and reliable source of income and ultimately contribute to these organizations having a much more positive impact in their different areas of work.

Building leadership and management skills

South Africa has a sufficient number of capacity-building NPOs and tertiary institutions to assist NPOs to meet the leadership challenges facing them. Thus it may not be necessary for donors to provide technical assistance through seconding staff. It is perhaps more appropriate for donors to support the training needs of NPOs by funding the training of staff in specific areas. It is particularly important to support the broadening of organizational management skills. Donors may also consider directly supporting local organizations that train NPOs to improve their fundraising strategies and that work to encourage and develop local philanthropy. One such organization is the National Foundation for Fundraising Training in Johannesburg, which works particularly with CBOs and black-run organizations.

Skills exchange

An interesting and beneficial form of skills exchange is exemplified by an arrangement that exists between the New Economics Foundation (NEF) in the UK and the Development Resources Centre (DRC) in South Africa. A staff member of the DRC works in London for three weeks with the NEF to build on the organizational development and strategic planning skills of NEF staff. In exchange an NEF staff member works at the DRC for three weeks a year to strengthen the DRC programmes dealing with indicators and social auditing.

Supporting innovation

In addition to the diversion of bilateral funds from the non-profit sector to government, there is an increased tendency for foreign donors to support charitable or welfare programmes rather than long-term development initiatives. Given that today's South Africa can be described as a veritable 'policy factory', and given that NPOs have a leading role to play in developing new policies and new pilot strategies for development, it is important that donors should support such pilot strategies. Successful new strategies and policies are beneficial in the long term as government may then build on them and replicate them on a larger scale.

Gazetteer

Many donors have one particular area of activity that they like to support. The Gazetteer section focuses on 11 separate areas. It looks at what is happening in each of these areas in South Africa today, what the particular needs are, and what role non-profit organizations are playing in meeting those needs.

- Education
- Arts and culture
- Health
- Social welfare
- Environment
- Rural development
- Housing
- Job creation
- Human rights
- Organizations that support the sector
- Women

Education

Transforming the education system is one of the biggest challenges facing South Africa. The government's policy recommendations in this area are underpinned by the objective of providing quality education for all. Given the decades of unequal provision of resources to the black population, this goal is going to take a long time to achieve and will need strong and effective action by all the actors involved in education.

According to statistics provided by the South African Institute of Race Relations, approximately 5 million people above the age of four years had had no education in 1994. Four million had a matriculation certificate only and 1.7 million had some form of post-matriculation. The rest of the population had had some education but had never matriculated.

The pass rate for matriculants in 1995 was 55 per cent. This average is low because for the first time the pass rates of black and white students from the various apartheid-driven educational institutions were aggregated. Provinces that had a large proportion of 'white' schools performed much better than is suggested by the national average. This indicates that government and other service providers need to ensure that a great part of the resources earmarked for education is directed to schools in the former oppressed communities.

Teacher education and redeployment

There is currently a perception that there are more teachers than can be absorbed by the various provincial education departments. Consequently, many teachers face the prospect of being redeployed from schools that are regarded as having sufficient teachers to schools that have a shortage of teachers. Those teachers who opt not to be redeployed for personal or other reasons may be made redundant. The government has already offered teachers voluntary retrenchment packages; this will mean the most experienced teachers leaving the sector because the packages are worthwhile only for teachers with more than ten years' experience. Organized teacher associations and unions are concerned at the effect this will have on the quality of teaching and education provision.

On the other hand, many NPOs in partnership with government are actively involved in upgrading the skills of teachers through in-service training. The development of teacher competence is regarded by South African educationalists as the key to meeting the government's goal of quality education for all.

Literacy and adult basic education

The National Literacy Cooperation (NLC) estimates that in 1994 about 15 million people in South Africa were functionally illiterate. Given these figures, the provision of adult basic education and training (ABET) is an important aspect of a national education campaign. The bulk of this work is done by organizations such as Project Literacy and Learn and Teach. Trade unions such as the National Union of Mineworkers (NUM) also play a significant role in ABET provision as a large proportion of mineworkers are functionally illiterate.

National Literacy Cooperation (NLC)

The NLC's aim is to promote literacy in South Africa so that as many people as possible can participate in the process of social transformation. It does this through campaigning for general recognition that adult basic education and training (ABET) is a critical component of development and by promoting high-quality ABET programmes in all nine provinces, with a particular emphasis on underdeveloped provinces.

The NLC runs ABET training courses throughout the country. It also runs training courses for ABET trainers and project staff, supports curriculum and materials development, and evaluates ABET training carried out by government and other NPOs.

The NLC's work focuses particularly on rural women, men and youth but it also works with urban-based people who have difficulties in reading and writing.

Contact Shirley Porota, PO Box 32485, Braamfontein 2017.
Tel +27 11 403 7657 *Fax* +27 11 711 2168
E-mail Shirley@NLC.wn.apc.org

Arts and culture

The government has recognized the key importance of arts and culture in enhancing the quality of life and promoting a suitable environment for creativity – and in developing human resources. An arts and culture programme will help in creating a unifying national identity and the government has pledged resources to this.

Private and corporate donors play an active role in the promotion of community theatre, dance, and arts and crafts. A number of award ceremonies are also held to encourage the growth of artistic and cultural skills.

Health

As with education and other basic services, the provision of health services has been characterized by racial disparities. Public health services have been inadequate and inaccessible for the majority of black South Africans. The government will not be able to provide the infrastructure and resources necessary to realize fully its vision of affordable health care for all South Africans. In some areas of the country health services for poor people may in fact decline owing to the policy of fiscal discipline and a desire to cut back on government spending over the next few years.

The government has made health care free to all children under the age of six and to pregnant women. This has benefited a large number of people but it has also put understaffed hospitals and clinics under enormous stresses, particularly in the rural areas.

Some of the major problems are related to a lack of qualified medical personnel in most of the rural areas. The National Health Department has employed doctors from Cuba and placed them in many of the most marginalized rural and urban communities. The employment of the Cuban doctors has generally been regarded as successful. However, owing to budgetary constraints and the adjustments that the government is introducing as part of its policy of fiscal discipline, health staff, including doctors and nurses, are being retrenched in many urban areas. The government is thus unable to increase its services and is instead reallocating resources from areas already in need of better services to areas with no health services. Gauteng province has been most seriously affected by these health cuts, which will inevitably have the most impact on the poor, who are dependent on public health services.

The role of NPOs

Clearly there are many gaps in health provision and NPOs have a major role to play throughout the country. Many health NPOs are, however, already finding it difficult to carry on their work, as donors tend to feel that basic health services should be the responsibility of the government. In the province of KwaZulu-Natal, NPOs working with and supporting community health workers are facing closure, even though those community health workers and their community health clinics are the only services available to many people. Donors need actively to support these community-based initiatives for health care.

Siyakha Trust

The Siyakha Trust is an NPO active in the province of KwaZulu-Natal. It has been training community health workers over the last five years and runs six health clinics. The key funder of the organization has been the European Union.

The Siyakha Trust has been struggling to do its work effectively over the last two years mainly because funders are cutting funds or diverting funds to government, whom they regard as having the responsibility to provide public heath care. The National Health Department, while acknowledging the importance of Siyakha, has not been providing funds to the organization. Siyakha is thus facing severe funding constraints at a time when the demand for its services is increasing.

Address PO Box 56534, Chatsworth 4030.
Tel +27 31 309 7999   *Fax* +27 31 309 7841

Social welfare

The 'residual' model of social welfare adopted in South Africa has ensured a 'partnership' between state and community-sponsored welfare initiatives. The model is characterized by minimal state intervention in the provision and financing of welfare services and social security, selective eligibility to receive services, and a focus upon helping individuals. Some of the services previously enjoyed only by whites (eg payment of rent for unemployed whites) have been cut back; the 'residue' of these funds is then used to provide other services.

Community-sponsored welfare organizations offer primarily rehabilitative social services and conduct some statutory work on behalf of the state. They are coordinated by national councils in various fields of service delivery. The national councils are NPOs, but in the past they worked very closely with government.

The role of NPOs

The non-profit sector has traditionally been seen as having an important role to play in welfare provision. This role has been recognized in practice through the inclusion of non-profit sector representatives in welfare decision-making structures and through a comprehensive system of state financial support for service provision by community-sponsored welfare organizations.

The major funding crisis that has afflicted South African NPOs has made welfare organizations less able to meet the enormous upsurge in the demand for services, resulting from the poverty, inequality and underdevelopment which affect so much of the country.

Environment

As in many developing countries, there is a tension between protecting the environment and development linked to job creation. This tension has been most pronounced in two of South Africa's most scenic areas, both key tourist attractions: St Lucia in KwaZulu-Natal and Saldanha Bay in the Western Cape. St Lucia was earmarked for mining and Saldanha Bay was identified as a site for a steel plant. Community advocacy involving the trade unions successfully put a stop to the development at St Lucia. On the other hand, the unions were key advocates for the development of the steel refinery at Saldanha Bay on the grounds that much-needed jobs would be created in the region.

The challenge in South Africa is to promote environmental protection as part of an economic development programme. Three aspects of environmental affairs that are given priority are conservation, tourism and population growth.

Developing eco-tourism

Tourism resources in South Africa have not been developed in a sustainable way to realize their full potential. The majority of South Africans have not been involved in tourism development and the economy has suffered accordingly because resources have not been effectively utilized.

Tourism needs to be developed into a strong and viable industry that will generate employment as well as contributing to the protection of the environment. The development of eco-tourism is therefore an important aspect of any programme to protect the environment, as it has the potential to link economic opportunities for poor communities with environmental protection measures.

Environmental education

The government has already recognized that environmental education is a vital element of all levels and programmes of the education and training system if South Africans are to become environmentally literate and enjoy a decent quality of life as a result of the sustainable use of resources. A number of NPOs are adopting an integrated approach towards environmental protection and stress the link between the workplace and the community when dealing with environmental issues.

They aim also to improve the attitude of business towards the environment.

The leading organization with regard to promoting 'developmental' eco-tourism and challenging government policies related to the environment is the Environmental Justice Networking Forum. The Forum has been championing the fight against moves by many Western countries to make South Africa the new dumping ground for toxic waste.

Environmental Justice Networking Forum (EJNF)

The EJNF brings together over 230 South African NPOs which subscribe to the values of environmental justice. They include women's, youth, rural, environmental and religious organizations and civics (residents' organizations), trade unions and service organizations.

The Forum works to strengthen and support action taken by poor communities and workers to address environmental injustices threatening their health and well-being. Besides challenging weak provisions in the country's laws that would have facilitated the move by European countries to negotiate a deal with the South African government whereby South Africa would 'manage' toxic waste, the Forum recently initiated a programme that would lead to greater NPO involvement in decision-making on environmental policy in South Africa.

Address PO Box 7110, Newtown 2113.
Tel +27 11 838 5449 *Fax* +27 11 838 7613

Rural development

Rural South Africa has suffered most from the socio-political policies of the past century. Millions of people were driven off their ancestral land and forced to live in 'Bantustans' (the former homelands of the apartheid era), which had little or no economic potential. Perhaps the most damaging of all the factors that contributed to the systematic underdevelopment in rural areas was the migrant labour system. With no possibilities for making a living in the barren land to which people were restricted, the men of thousands of households left the rural areas to work and live in the urban areas. Most of the money earned was spent in the urban areas, resulting in little benefit for workers' families. In effect the migrant labour system reduced the rural areas to poverty-stricken pools of cheap labour for the mines and other urban industries.

Land restitution

Land restitution is therefore central both to stability and to any broadening out of the economic potential of the rural areas of South Africa. A Land Claims Commission has been established by the government to facilitate land transfers. To date 11,000 claims have been made by people hoping to get back land that they were forced off.

The National Land Committee, an organization committed to genuine land restitution, is concerned

National Land Committee

The National Land Committee originated as the National Committee against Removals, established in 1985 to support communities affected by the then National Party government's policy of forced removals. It is a network of land service and advocacy organizations, which recognizes the enduring legacy of apartheid. The Committee is committed to the promotion of social justice in South Africa in relation to access to and control over land and related resources. Of particular concern to the National Land Committee are the victims of forced removals. These include farmworkers, labour tenants (people who work and live on a farm), residents of informal settlements and women.

Address PO Box 30944, Braamfontein 2017.
Tel +27 11 403 3803 *Fax* +27 11 339 6315
E-mail NLC@wn.apc.org

that land claims are not being processed fast enough. Of the 10,000 claims that had been lodged by August 1996, only 648 have been formally acknowledged by government through its gazette. Of these only one has been forwarded to the Land Claims Court, but it was rejected by the court for technical reasons. Rural and other dispossessed communities will still need to struggle to get their land for many years to come, and organizations such as the National Land Committee are going to need support in championing these struggles.

The land reform programme, combining asset redistribution with enhancement of tenure, has an important role to play in improving the long-term prospects for employment and income generation in the rural economy. Progress has been made to finalize procedures for the rapid release of land and the introduction of settlement grants. Complementary initiatives include emergent farmer support programmes. Over time, agricultural development associated with land reform will play a key role in facilitating the redistribution of income and economic activity.

Water and sanitation

Improved water and sanitation is the first priority of rural communities. Rapid progress in providing a supply of drinkable water to the 12 million people without adequate access will be a major contribution to poverty relief.

Mvula Trust

The Mvula Trust is an organization committed to improving the health and welfare of disadvantaged rural and semi-urban South Africans through improved access to safe water and sanitation. The Trust provides financial assistance and other forms of support to projects which increase the access of poor communities to safe water and sanitation and strengthen local capacity to manage water and sanitation services. It is committed to implementing 500 projects costing R1.5 billion (US$325 million).

Address PO Box 32351, Braamfontein 2017.
Tel +27 11 403 3425   *Fax* +27 11 403 1260

Housing

South Africa is experiencing a housing crisis, with an estimated housing backlog (a shortfall in relation to planned delivery) of 1.5 million homes. The situation is exacerbated by the fact that there are 200,000 more families in need of housing each year. Low government expenditure on housing during the 1980s, the recession and low growth rate of that period, and the resultant downsizing within the construction sector served to heighten this crisis.

In 1993 an estimated 50,000 formal housing units were delivered. In 1994 the rate of delivery fell to just under 20,000 units. In contrast to this is the extraordinarily high rate of delivery of informal housing (shacks and other forms of housing that are not considered to be permanent). The National Housing Forum, a policy body bringing together government agencies, private sector institutions and NPOs, estimates that only 66 per cent of housing units in South Africa are built of permanent building materials.

What this means is that while the formal housing delivery sector gears up over the next five years, people will still be meeting their housing needs informally. The government's policy of 'incremental housing' is partially designed to support this phenomenon. An essential component of this scheme is that people will be given housing subsidies to erect a small dwelling. As individual owners get the means, they can then extend their homes through accessing the formal financial institutions. The problem with this approach is that while approximately 80 per cent of the working population will qualify for government subsidies (ie people earning less than R3,500 a month – approximately US$780), between 40 and 70 per cent of the country's population will not have access to the loans needed to extend their homes (ie households earning less than R1,500 ($335) per month).

While it is argued that the incremental approach to housing will boost the efforts of people who are willing to build their own homes and over time overcome housing constraints, this policy mainly benefits people with a reasonable source of income.

The housing problem cannot be solved by public provision in the foreseeable future: though government has increased housing's share of the national budget from 1.5 per cent in 1994/95 to 3.4 per cent in 1995/96, this increased budget will still not meet housing requirements nationally.

The key need of the housing sector is therefore an extensive loan guarantee scheme and innovative savings programmes for low-income earners: many contractors are pulling out of the low-income housing sector because of the banks' refusal to grant finance for these homes. Establishing community foundations may also help in the funding of local housing programmes and other community development projects.

Job creation

Over the past decade, employment growth in the formal sectors of the economy has stagnated and private sector employment has fallen. Since the 1970s, unregulated low-wage employment has increased significantly; a large pool of unemployed men and women who earn no income or derive sporadic earnings from informal self-employment makes up about one-third of the potential workforce.

Irregular, subcontracted or part-time workers employed on semi-formal contractual terms are becoming the preferred source of labour for many employers. This is resulting in a growing gap between wages and benefits in the regulated and unregulated parts of the labour market. Where regulations increase the costs of job creation, employers turn to unregulated forms of employment.

Two structural features that affect employment can be noted:

- Apartheid-based migrant labour flows have evolved into more complex rural–urban linkages, both between urban and rural households and involving longer-term migration. The pace of urbanization has been slower than observers were predicting a decade ago; this is consistent with the slow rate of formal sector job creation.

- Government has contributed disproportionately to job creation over the past decade; public sector job creation has somewhat exceeded the average growth of the labour force since the early 1980s. Services have become an increasingly important source of employment; indeed, they are the only sector outside government in which employment growth has continued during the 1990s.

The role of NPOs

A number of NPOs have devoted themselves to capacity-building as well as acting as facilitators between companies and unemployed people. The main areas of training are technical, for example handicrafts and carpentry; training is also offered in general business skills. An increasing number of people are setting up their own businesses. However, a number of laws hamper the ability of people to be enterprising and constrain small businesses from growing and making a real contribution to the job creation process in South Africa.

Human rights

South Africa arguably has one of the most progressive constitutions in the world. The Bill of Rights enshrines the right to freedom of information and association and the right to life. The rights of individuals in South Africa are protected and discrimination on all grounds, including discrimination on the basis of sexual preference, is outlawed.

A Human Rights Commission has been established to monitor human rights abuses by the state and other sectors in society as well as to introduce programmes that would enhance the human rights of vulnerable sectors of society, particularly the poor. The irony is that although the government established the Human Rights Commission, it is chronically underfunded.

The underfunding of the Commission is symptomatic of a broader attitude shift on the part of many local and foreign donors, which are cutting back on funding human rights organizations and their activities now that a democratic government is in place. Thus organizations such as the Black Sash, which have championed human rights issues over the last 30 years, have had to cut down on their activities.

Other contentious issues relating to human rights are whether the death penalty, which was abolished with the advent of democracy, should be reintroduced in an effort to reduce the crime rate. Anti-abortion groups are planning to test the constitutionality of legal abortion against the backdrop of the 'Right to Life' clause in the South African constitution.

Black Sash

The Black Sash is one of the oldest human rights organizations in the country, and it has an international reputation. It was set up in 1955 in protest against the constitutional manipulations which led to the removal of coloured voters in the Cape from the common voters role. Constitutional issues have remained a major concern from that time until the present.

The Black Sash took a leading role in opposing the pass laws, which attempted to keep the cities of South Africa 'white' while pushing black South Africans into the poverty-stricken 'bantustans'. This involved a massive population resettlement programme and the 'denationalization' of 8 million people.

The Black Sash now works to promote the constitutional entrenchment and protection by law of human rights for all South Africans, equal access to justice for all, and the establishment of democratic and accountable government. Its priorities at the present time are social security, in its widest meaning, and the implementation of the socio-economic rights set out in the new Constitution of 1996. The Black Sash has a particular focus on women. It is also currently involved in efforts to protect the rights of illegal and legal immigrants in an environment where xenophobia is rising, particularly against immigrants from other African countries.

In 1994 the Black Sash suffered its own funding crisis when USAID stopped its funding without any notice whatsoever, and without giving any reasons. At the same time money owed by the EU was delayed in transfer for many months owing to bureaucratic procedures in Brussels and Paris. Fortunately the Black Sash was able to survive the crisis through the support of its other long-term donors and because it was able to widen its donor base to include a variety of other foundations and trusts.

The Black Sash continues to operate advice centres in eight different cities in the country; it is also seeking to extend its paralegal training and outreach programmes to rural areas and small towns. It has an extensive parliamentary monitoring programme and, from this base of hands-on hard work, continues to defend constitutional government and to promote a culture of human rights.

Contact Sheena Duncan, 4th Floor, 12 Plein Street, Cape Town 8001.
Tel +27 21 461 7804 *Fax* +27 21 461 8004
E-mail sduncan@wn.apc.org

Organizations that support the sector

There are a number of NPOs whose role is to support and strengthen the non-profit sector as a whole. Their work includes provision of information and consultancy services, carrying out policy research work and encouraging philanthropic giving.

There are approximately 55 forums and networks of non-profit organizations. These networks and forums range from forums such as the National Recycling Forum to development-oriented networks such as the Urban Sector Network, which brings together NPOs working on urban development and housing. Although there is no single 'umbrella body' for NPOs, the South African National NGO Coalition emerged in 1995 as a national network incorporating provincial coalitions and sectoral networks.

Women

The fundamental shift in South Africa that has major implications for women is that equality and non-sexism have become one of the country's priorities. Government departments at national, provincial and local level, in areas such as finance, land, housing, health, justice, trade and industry, water and forestry, education and security, have to ensure that staff programmes and resources are oriented towards empowering the most oppressed and exploited South Africans: black working-class women.

The concept of gender and power in South Africa has not been adequately addressed in terms of the way in which it is linked with race and class. The category 'women' should be regarded in the same way as categories such as the 'aged', the 'disabled' or 'rural'. If women are to be able to participate effectively in society, the obstacles they face must be recognized. The state must take responsibility for developing women's potential and skills and recognizing their existing skills so that they can effectively take positions of leadership.

South African National NGO Coalition

The South African National NGO Coalition was launched in August 1995. It is in fact a 'network of networks' as it brings together nine provincial coalitions and several sectoral or issue-based networks.

The Coalition is committed to working for a strong non-profit sector. It seeks to promote participatory democracy and people-centred development.

It is a voluntary body comprising willing participant organizations that are represented in sectoral networks or provincial coalitions and which operate according to an agreed set of values and principles. It will not, however, play a role in the administration of funding to member organizations.

The functions of the Coalition are to:

- foster an enabling environment for NPOs in interactions with government, business and donors;
- provide a forum for information-sharing and advocacy on a range of issues of concern to its members;
- facilitate international networking that will be beneficial to its members;
- ensure that members observe the obligations laid down by the Coalition, including financial accountability and effective service delivery;
- create an enabling legislative and structural environment for NPOs;
- rebuild the human resources of the non-profit sector, developing skills in the areas of fundraising, strategic and operational planning, financial management, advocacy and lobbying, human resources management and policy development;
- reduce operating costs and develop the financial sustainability of the non-profit sector.

Under the new Executive Director, Kumi Naidoo, the Coalition is focusing particularly on financial and sustainability issues – ranging from ways of reducing costs (such as, for example, negotiating special rates from hotels and airlines) to building capital for the sector through investment services in cooperation with outside financial institutions.

Contact Kumi Naidoo, 4 Melridge, 56 Stiemens Street, Braamfontein 2001. *Tel* +27 11 403 7746 *Fax* +27 11 403 8703 *E-mail* NGOCOAL@sn.apc.org

Useful organizations

Access
Multi-disciplinary non-profit development organization providing practical training programmes on all aspects of development.
Address PO Box 17181, Congella 4013.
Tel +27 31 25 8266 *Fax* +27 31 25 4938

Alexandra Health Centre
Almost the only provider of health care in Alexandra township, north of Johannesburg. It provides a 24-hour emergency unit, adult and paediatric outpatient departments and outreach services including satellite clinics.
Contact Nomvuyo Molefe, PO Box 175, Bergvlei 2012.
Tel +27 11 440 1231 *Fax* +27 11 887 9007

ANANZI – The South African Search Engine
General Internet search engine for South Africa.
Web address http://www.ananzi.co.za

Anglo American and De Beers Chairman's Fund
Anglo American is South Africa's largest corporate donor; it supports any cause or project which it consider to be socially constructive.
Contact M C Keeton, 44 Main Street,
PO Box 61587, Marshalltown 2107.
Tel +27 11 638 9111 *Fax* +27 11 638 4998

Black Sash
One of South Africa's oldest human rights organizations, Black Sash works to promote human rights for all South Africans, equal access to justice for all and the establishment of democratic and accountable government.
Contacts Allison Tilley/Sheena Duncan, 5 Long Street,
Mowbray 7700. *Tel* +27 21 685 3513 *Fax* +27 21 685 7510

Community Chest of the Western Cape
The oldest and largest of South Africa's Community Chests, it distributes some R10 million annually to over 300 welfare bodies in the Western Cape. Programmes focus on family and child welfare services, services for physically and mentally handicapped people, and rehabilitation and health care support.
Contact Amelia Jones, Borwick House,
PO Box 3836, 82 Bree Street, Cape Town.
Tel +27 21 24 3344 *Fax* +27 21 24 7387
Web address http://www.cia.co.za/cchest

Community Development Resource Association
Provides capacity-building, counselling and organizational development and evaluation services to NGOs and CBOs in South Africa. Organizes workshops and develops learning materials.
Contact Allan Kaplan, PO Box 221, Woodstock 7915.
Tel +27 21 448 8080 *Fax* +27 21 47 9006

Development Bank of South Africa
Paragovernmental funding agency. Activities include education and training; rural and agricultural development information; institutional development and capacity-building; urban development.
Contact Marius Schoon, PO Box 1234, Halfway House 1685.
Tel +27 11 313 3911 *Fax* +27 11 313 3086

Development Resources Centre
Activities include organizational development and capacity-building, research, advocacy, information, training, fundraising and alternatives to grant finance, and using effectiveness indicators.
Contact Gavin Andersson, PO Box 6079, Johannesburg 2000.
Tel +27 11 838 7504 *Fax* +27 11 838 6310
E-mail DRC@wn.apc.org

Environmental Justice Networking Forum
Brings together over 230 South African NPOs which subscribe to the values of environmental justice. They include women's, youth, rural, environmental and religious organizations and civics (residents' organizations), trade unions and service organizations.
Address PO Box 7110, Newtown 2113.
Tel +27 11 838 5449 *Fax* +27 11 838 7613

Ford Foundation
Funds and supports: law and human rights, higher education, community economic development, public policy.
Contact John Gerhart, PO Box 30953, Braamfontein 2017.
Tel +27 11 403 5912 *Fax* +27 11 403 1575

Foundation for Welfare and Charity Support
Funding agency; main interests are information technology, fundraising, education and the environment.
Contact Peter Hayward, Private Bag X8, Bryanston 2021
Tel/Fax +27 11 442 5675

Independent Development Trust
Raises money and finances projects without government interference, and provides the poor with access to credit throughout South Africa. IDT believes it should become a permanent institution, independent of government.
Contact Dr Shalto Cross, PO Box 16114, Vlaeberg 8018.
Tel +27 21 23 8030 *Fax* +27 21 23 4512

Interfund
A consortium of European donors. Funded activities include development management training; non-formal education; urban development and local government training; community health and AIDS awareness projects; women and gender development.
Contact Barry Smith, PO Box 32340, Braamfontein 2017.
Tel +27 11 403 2966 *Fax* +27 11 339 2740

Joint Education Trust (JET)
Launched with a commitment of R500 million from 20 of South Africa's largest companies, JET's aim is to improve the quality of education, focusing on the development of the poorest communities.
Contact Hugh McLean, PO Box 178, Wits 2050.
Tel/Fax +27 11 339 3212

Kagiso Trust
Funds mainly general education, community and civic development programmes, health and youth. Does not fund housing or services that central government should provide.
Contact Horst Kleinschmidt, PO Box 1878, Johannesburg 2000. *Tel* +27 11 403 7714
Fax +27 11 403 1940

Kagiso Trust Investments (KTI)
A separate business venture set up by the Kagiso Trust; the aims of KTI are the empowerment of the black community and the generation of funds for the Kagiso Trust.
Contact Eric Molobi, PO Box 3528, Rivonia 2128.
Tel +27 11 807 1106 *Fax* +27 11 807 6379

Kwazulu-Natal and National CBO Network
Network of community development organizations working on income generation and job creation projects through the following skills: sewing, agriculture, handicrafts, beadwork, pottery, youth projects.
Contact Jane Ngobese, c/o UEDP UD, PO Box X10, Dalbridge 4014.
Tel +27 31 260 1492/503 1206
Fax +27 31 260 1340 (Natal U)

Charles Stewart Mott Foundation
Funds and supports education for democratic participation; supports women's participation in government and non-government organizations; strengthens the effectiveness of the non-profit sector.
Contact Christa Kuljian, PO Box 32088, Braamfontein 2017.
Tel +27 11 403 6934 *Fax* +27 11 403 7566

Mvula Trust
Committed to improving the health and welfare of disadvantaged rural and semi-urban South Africans through improved access to safe water and sanitation.
Address PO Box 32351, Braamfontein 2017.
Tel +27 11 403 3425 *Fax* +27 11 403 1260

National Foundation for Fundraising Training
Works particularly with CBOs and black-run organizations to improve their fundraising strategies.
Contact Jo Rhodes, PO Box 94106, Yeoville 2143.
Tel +27 11 484 1460 *Fax* +27 11 484 4235
E-mail NFFT@ Bridges.co.za

National Housing Forum
A policy body bringing together government agencies, private sector institutions and NPOs.
Address PO Box 1115, Johannesburg 2000.
Tel +27 11 838 5449 *Fax* +27 11 838 1855

National Land Committee
A network of land service and advocacy organizations, committed to the promotion of social justice in relation to access to and control over land and related resources; particularly concerned with the victims of forced removals.
Address PO Box 30944, Braamfontein 2017.
Tel +27 11 403 3803 *Fax* +27 11 339 6315
E-mail NLC@wn.apc.org

National Literacy Cooperation (NLC)
Promotes adult basic education and training (ABET), which it sees as a critical component of development, with an emphasis on underdeveloped provinces.
Contact Shirley Porota, PO Box 32485, Braamfontein 2017.
Tel +27 11 403 7657 *Fax* +27 11 711 2168
E-mail Shirley@NLC.wn.apc.org

National Progressive Primary Health Care Network (NPPHCN)
Promotes primary health care through campaigning for public policies that will result in better health care for South Africa's poor and marginalized communities.
Address PO Box 32095, Braamfontein 2017.
Tel +27 11 403 4647 *Fax* +27 11 403 1832
E-mail PPHCNJHB@wn.apc.org

National Welfare, Social Service and Development Forum (NWSSDF)
Activities: welfare, social services, forum policy.
Address PO Box 4025, Johannesburg 2000.
Tel +27 11 836 6160 *Fax* +27 11 836 6034
E-mail trakhetla@ bringes.co.za

Open Society Foundation for South Africa
Committed to promoting the values, institutions
and practices of an open, civil and democratic society,
not dominated by the state, in which minorities and
divergent opinions are respected.
Contact Michael Savage, Colinton House, Norwich Oval,
1 Oakdale Road, Newlands 7700, PO Box 23161,
Claremont 7735. *Tel* +27 21 683 3489 *Fax* +27 21 683 3550
E-mail osfsa@aztec.co.za

Operation Hunger
One of the biggest NPOs in the country, dedicated to
alleviating malnutrition and poverty. It has seven regional
offices, with a national head office in Johannesburg.
Contact P Davids, PO Box 32257, Braamfontein 2017.
Tel +27 11 403 6750 *Fax* +27 11 403 1386

Oxfam (UK and Ireland)
Funds rural communities dispossessed of their land, with
a focus on farm workers and their families. It does crisis
work throughout South Africa, particularly in KwaZulu-
Natal, the Eastern Cape and Northern Province.
Contact Nigel Taylor, PO Box 31009, Braamfontein 2017.
Tel +27 11 339 2560/81 *Fax* +27 11 339 2740
E-mail oxfam@praxis.co.za

Programme for Development Research, PRODDER – HSRC
Development information medium, responsible for
disseminating information on all aspects of development
to development organizations and practitioners in South
Africa and abroad.
Contact David Barnard, PO Box 32410, Braamfontein 2017.
Tel +27 11 339 4451 *Fax* +27 11 403 2353

Sached Trust (South African Council on Higher Education)
Adult education and training development organization,
facilitating distance and community learning schemes
and providing curriculum support in schools.
Address PO Box 11350, Johannesburg 2000.
Tel +27 11 333 9746 *Fax* +27 11 333 2297

SANGONet
Electronic e-mail and Internet server; focuses on
development information.
Contact Anriette Esterhuysen,
PO Box 31, Johannesburg 2000. *Tel* +27 11 838 6943
Fax +27 11 492 1058 *Web address* http://wn.apc.org

Siyakha Trust
Trains community health workers and runs six health
clinics.
Address PO Box 56534, Chatsworth 4030.
Tel +27 31 309 7999 *Fax* +27 31 309 7841

South African Communication Service (SACS)
Internet server with detailed information about the
government and economy. A searchable database contains
over 55,000 articles and transcripts from the last two years.
Web address http://www.sacs.org.za

South African Grantmakers Association (SAGA)
Works to facilitate networks between funders and
communities; to channel more funding into development
particularly from the business sector as part of corporate
social responsibility programmes.
Address PO Box 10499, Johannesburg 2000.
Tel +27 11 403 1610 *Fax* +27 11 408 3998

South African National NGO Coalition
A 'network of networks', bringing together nine provincial
coalitions and nine sectoral or issue-based networks. It aims
to foster an enabling environment for NPOs in interactions
with government, business and donors, and to provide
a forum for information-sharing and advocacy on a range
of issues.
National Office *Contact* Kumi Naidoo, 4 Melridge,
56 Stiemens Street, Braamfontein 2001. *Tel* +27 11 403 7746
Fax +27 11 403 8703 *E-mail* NGOCOAL@sn.apc.org
Executive Committee *Contact* Rams Ramashia,
PO Box 32286, Braamfontein 2017.
Tel +27 11 403 3010 *Fax* +27 11 403 1104

Transitional National Development Trust (TNDT)
Funds education, health, rural development, urban
development, small, medium and micro-enterprise
development, good governance and democracy.
Contact Paul Jackson, PO Box 31959, Braamfontein 2017.
Tel +27 11 403 6650 *Fax* +27 11 403 2515

Urban Sector Network
Brings together NPOs working on urban development
and housing.
Address PO Box 32707, Braamfontein 2017.
Tel +27 11 403 3835 *Fax* +27 11 339 7762

About CAF

Other publications from CAF

CAF, Charities Aid Foundation, is a registered charity with a unique mission – to increase the substance of charity in the UK and overseas. It provides services that are both charitable and financial which help donors make the most of their giving and charities make the most of their resources.

Many of CAF's publications reflect the organization's purpose: *Dimensions of the Voluntary Sector* offers the definitive financial overview of the sector, while *The Directory of Grant Making Trusts* provides the most comprehensive source of funding information available.

As an integral part of its activities, CAF works to raise standards of management in voluntary organizations. This includes the making of grants by its own Grants Council, sponsorship of the Charity Annual Report and Accounts Awards, seminars, training courses and the Charities Annual Conference, the largest regular gathering of key people from within the voluntary sector. In addition, Charitynet is now established as the leading Internet site on voluntary action.

For decades, CAF has led the way in developing tax-effective services to donors, and these are now used by more than 150,000 individuals and 2,000 of the UK's leading companies. Many are also using CAF's CharityCard, the world's first debit card designed exclusively for charitable giving. CAF's unique range of investment and administration services for charities includes the CafCash High Interest Cheque Account, two common investment funds for longer-term investment and a full appeals and subscription management service.

CAF's activities are not limited to the UK, however. Increasingly, CAF is looking to apply the same principles and develop similar services internationally, in its drive to increase the substance of charity across the world.

Dimensions of the Voluntary Sector

How is the voluntary sector changing?
Editor **Cathy Pharoah**
Published annually in June

An easy-to-use storehouse of facts, figures and critical thinking, *Dimensions of the Voluntary Sector* provides up-to-date information on the 'third sector', which brings in over £10 billion and employs 400,000 people.

The definitive publication on the income and resources of the voluntary sector in the UK, it is widely regarded as an essential tool for busy managers, practitioners and academic researchers alike.

Completely redesigned in order to present statistics in an easily accessible and attractive form, among other topics, it includes data on:

- the top fundraising charities;
- the top corporate donors;
- the top grant-making trusts;
- the patterns in National Lottery funding.

Other, more specialized tables analyse the performance of NHS trusts, local authority support for charities and fundraising through charity shops.

The Non-Profit Sector in the UK

1st edition
ISBN 1859340377 £9.95
Published July 1997

This retrospective overview has been written for everyone interested in the role, activities and public profile of the non-profit sector in the UK in 1996. It provides a commentary on the major issues and events which have shaped the past 12 months for British non-profit organizations and assesses the impact on their work.

Supported by extensive background material on the legal and fiscal framework within which non-profit organizations operate, the distinguished authors examine the key developments in the political, social and economic arenas.

Among many others, topics addressed include the transfer of the VSU to the Department of National Heritage, the publication of the 'Deakin' report on the future of the sector and the changing role of volunteering.

Comprehensive coverage of fundraising issues, including the continuing debate surrounding the impact of the National Lottery and the growing importance of trading, is also provided.

The Non-Profit Sector in India

Michael Norton
ISBN 1859340237 £15.00
Published August 1996

The Non-Profit Sector in Russia

Paul LeGendre
ISBN 1859340369 £15.00
Published April 1997

The *Non-Profit Sector in . . .* series is designed to provide readers with an introductory overview of voluntary activity in a particular country or region.

Each title appearing in the series includes:

- a review of the history and development of the non-profit sector
- an introduction to the political, economic and social environment
- an evaluation of the current situation of the local sector, including information on:
- main areas of activity
- funding sources
- relationships with local and national government
- principal needs and challenges
- an examination of the potential role of foreign donors
- a look at the challenges facing the different parts of the local sector

Published as a resource for corporate and foundation supporters of civil society and participatory development, the series paints an objective picture of the evolving sector across the globe. Written in an accessible, 'journalistic' style, the reports will enable even the busiest executives to acquire a rapid understanding of the key facts they need to inform their judgement.

HIV & AIDS in Russia

Darren Headley
ISBN 1859340156 £15.00
Published March 1996

Russia remained relatively isolated from the dramatic worldwide spread of HIV and AIDS in the early 1980s. However, since the collapse of communism a sexual revolution has taken place and the country is now confronting what some classify as the early stages of an epidemic.

HIV & AIDS in Russia highlights the flaws in the official response and illustrates the manner in which the emerging non-profit sector has stepped in to provide the support so desperately needed by sufferers, their families and the community at large.

Homelessness in Russia

Alexei Bodungen
ISBN 1859340075 £12.95
Published 1994

This report brings the plight of Russia's homeless people, often characterized as outcasts or criminals, sharply into focus. It illustrates the potential for change and the obstacles which exist in Russian society.

The Voluntary Sector in the European Union

The legal and fiscal framework
Harry Kidd
ISBN 185934030X £15.00
October 1996

This book provides a simple bird's-eye view of the legal and fiscal framework within which associations, foundations and charities operate in EU member states. Topics covered in Part One include: the common characteristics of voluntary organizations within the EU; the legal and cultural differences between member states; relevant international agreements; the VAT regime.

Part Two gives a country-by-country outline of the types of voluntary organization found in each member state and of the fiscal treatment both of voluntary organizations and of gifts and donors.

Index